Sex and Cognition

Doreen Kimura

A Bradford Book
The MIT Press
Cambridge, Massachusetts
London, England

First MIT Press paperback edition, 2000
© 1999 Massachusetts Institute of Technology

This book was set in Sabon by Northeastern Graphic Services, Inc., and was printed and bound in the United States of America.

Library of Congress Cataloging-in-Publication Data
Kimura, Doreen.
    Sex and cognition / Doreen Kimura.
      p.   cm.
    "A Bradford book."
    Includes bibliographical references and index.
    ISBN 0-262-11236-1 (hardcover : alk. paper), 0-262-61164-3 (pb)
    1. Cognition. 2. Sex differences (Psychology) 3. Sex
differences. I. Title.
BF311.K485 1999
153.3'3—dc21
                                            98-26802
                                              CIP

10 9 8 7 6 5 4

For Charlotte

Contents

Preface

My aim in this book is to provide an intelligible overview of the field of sex differences in cognition for the educated nonspecialist. The book is not intended as an exhaustive reference work on the subject, though I believe it presents all the major findings. Some readers may not find it necessary to read the background contained in chapters 2 and 3 before moving on to the rest of the book. An elementary review of the standard procedures used in dealing with numbers is provided in the appendix. Readers unfamiliar with concepts like standard deviation, effect sizes, correlation, and so on, may consult this appendix. Chapter 12, on body asymmetry, can be skipped without losing any essential information about sex differences in cognition.

The reader will find that much of the human research referred to in this book was conducted in my own laboratory at the University of Western Ontario. I have certainly not intended to omit important work from other labs, and have not, I hope, done so. But we always know more about the research we are personally involved in, so the tendency to feel a sense of familiarity and security with the results is inevitably greater. Relying heavily on this work has also allowed me to provide more personal commentary about the studies than I could have done with others' research.

Most of the research done in my lab was supported by the Medical Research Council and the Natural Sciences and Engineering Research Council of Canada.

It is a pleasure to acknowledge my many collaborators in this research, former graduate students or post-doctoral fellows. They include Elizabeth

Hampson, Neil Watson, Jeff Hall, Diana Ingram, Jonathan Lomas, Jeannette McGlone, Diane Lunn, Catherine Gouchie, Liisa Galea, Rhonda Peterson, Karen Nicholson, Tom James, David Collins, Karen Chipman, Kathryn Stokes, and Deborah Saucier.

A number of people read the manuscript in whole or in part. I am especially grateful to Neil Watson and Charlotte Vanderwolf for their detailed comments on the entire work. Jeff Hall and Karen Nicholson also made useful comments on parts of the manuscript and Tom James was responsible for many of the figures and for some of the data analyses.

Sex and Cognition

1

Introduction

When science ignores facts in favour of ideology . . . it ceases to be science and becomes propaganda for a dogma.
Kenneth Hilborn, 1996

This book will describe the major differences between men and women in cognitive or problem-solving abilities. It will also discuss the possible biological contributions to such differences. Many social scientists claim that it is unnecessary to invoke biological factors at all in explaining how people come to differ in their cognitive patterns. They prefer to attribute the variation that we see in human beings to variations in environmental, including socialization, influences. An extreme version of this position insists that unless a cognitive function or the relevant brain system shows sex differences at birth, we can never infer that it was not environmentally determined. For example, it has been suggested that, since newborn babies can neither do math nor hit a target accurately, we may not infer that these behaviors are influenced by biological factors (Foss 1996).

Let's consider how we would understand the development of a physiological function like lactation—the production of milk by the mammary glands—within such a framework. Lactation normally does not occur in children of either sex. Nor does it occur in adult males; but it begins in adult females after the birth of a child. Must we then conclude that it is determined by the different social environments that males and females experience? Hardly! It is equally fallacious, therefore, to claim that behavioral sex differences that make their appearance after childhood must be solely, or even primarily, due to gendered socialization.

Similarly, some writers insist that ability differences between men and women must be considered experientially determined unless we can demonstrate unequivocally that they are not. For example, "I impose the highest standards of *proof* . . . on claims about biological inequality." (Fausto-Sterling 1992) This is surely a very strange approach. It implies that we may not entertain biological explanations of human behavior until we have ruled out all plausible socialization mechanisms. To illustrate how strange this viewpoint is, we might turn the argument around and say we will not accept a difference between the sexes as environmentally influenced unless we can rule out the possibility that the differences are congenital. This is as logically acceptable as the first position, and equally flawed. The aim of scientific research is not (or should not be) to uphold or deny any particular social or political ideology. Rather, the aim in science must be to find the truest explanation we can; that is, the explanation that best fits all the current facts, regardless of current dogma.

If we want to develop an accurate account of how people's problem-solving behaviors originate, we cannot, a priori, willfully exclude any potential source of variation across individuals. It is not only unjustified scientifically to take such a biased view of how behaviors are determined, it is contrary to common sense. The business of science is to find out how the world really works, not how it ought to work according to some wishful schema or other. Scientific explanations change as more information comes in, but at any one point in time a scientific analysis attempts to encompass *all* relevant facts. In human cognition, this must include data from biologically relevant sources such as hormonal and brain research and studies in nonhuman species.

This does not require us to give equal consideration to all possible interpretations of a given finding. For example, an isolated fact, such as that women in one study remembered landmarks on a particular learned route better than men did, could be due to any number of factors. It could be due to women's better overall memory for objects (though this explanation can be ruled out by giving a separate item-memory test and seeing if the general memory accounts for the better landmark memory). It could also be due to the fact that particular items on the route—a red schoolhouse, a specific tree—hold greater interest for women; but if this sex difference holds up across several studies in which the landmarks differ, this is an unlikely explanation. Other possibilities may come to mind. The most probable explanation, however, in the absence of contradictory data, is that this is part of a general mammalian pattern that is also seen in rodents. That is, it is probably due to a strategy, favored by females, to use unique items in their environment to find their way.

Egalitarian Ideology

The bias against biological explanation seems to have arisen from egalitarian ideologies that confuse the Western concept of equal treatment before the law—the societal application of the idea that "all men are created equal"—with the claim that all people are in fact equal. People are not born equal in strength, health, temperament, or intelligence. This is simply a fact of life no sensible person can deny. We have chosen a system of governance which has decided that *despite such inequalities* each individual shall have an equal right to just treatment before the law, as well as equal opportunity.

Egalitarian ideology, however, often goes beyond this and insists that all people would be equal if they had equal environmental stimulation. That is, if upbringing, nurturance, exposure to education, opportunity, and so forth were exactly the same for everyone (a situation in practice impossible to achieve, hence impossible to test), we would all be equally endowed. Apart from the appalling dullness our lives would suffer, this is such nonsense that it is difficult to see how anyone can maintain it with a straight face. Most of us have grown up with brothers and sisters who have shared most aspects of our environment, yet we turned out quite different. We all have friends with backgrounds similar to our own, yet here the diversity in temperament, skills, and ultimate occupation is often greater. A social scientist flatly unwilling to entertain the idea that there are important biological contributions to the variations we see in cognitive pattern from one person to another has stopped being a scientist and has become an ideologue.

It has been suggested that a distinguishing characteristic of ideology is its commitment to a position, regardless of evidence (Hilborn 1996). Sexism, racism, and egalitarianism can all be considered ideologies to the extent that they are commitments to a system of beliefs *without empirical support*.

Nature/Nurture

What form, then, should scientific explanations of differences between the sexes take? It has become apparent over the years that the nature/nurture argument in its polarized form is an unprofitable one, since genetic predispositions cannot operate in a vacuum and environments must have a genetic code to work on. In other words, there can be no explanation that entirely rules out either environmental or genetic influences. In fact, even the basic dichotomy implied here is too simple. Factors such as sex hormones, variation in which is indirectly due to genetic factors, may in some sense be considered as environmental in nature. The potential complexity of such determinants of behavior is indicated by the fact that the amount and type of sex hormones can vary significantly depending on other prenatal influences present—stress, general health, nutrition, and so forth.

Insofar as natural selection arises out of the past environment of a species, any species' genetic characteristics are inevitably constrained by such environments. Indeed, one might expect the genetic code to develop the typical phenotype only in supportive environments, that is, environments similar to those in which the genetic code evolved. Some general characteristics of the external world, such as the circadian cycle and the dimensionality of space, have remained the same for millions of years (Shepard 1987). These characteristics may therefore in some way be encoded in the genetic makeup of most living organisms. Different genetic characteristics would be required of animals who are mobile on land, as compared to water, and so on. In other words, we should expect a match between the genetic code of a species and its past environment.

So the activation of genes is often environmentally determined. Yet for any influence of the environment to have a lasting effect, there must be a permanent physiological change of some kind.

The *Oxford Dictionary of Biology* defines biology as "the study of living organisms, which includes their structure, . . . functioning, origin and evolution." So when we talk of biological influences we are referring to a very broad spectrum of factors including, for example, our evolutionary legacy as social beings. Many people assume that to label a process *biological* rules out substantial modification to that process in the course of one's life, but this is incorrect. For example, if a certain level of androgens (masculinizing sex hormones) early in life is optimal for organizing the brain for certain spatial functions in later life, we should not assume that this influence is fixed or unalterable. Two individuals with the same degree of exposure to androgens prenatally may experience many other interacting "biological" influences that might make their performance on a spatial test different. In fact, the idea that any two individuals will have exactly the same degree of exposure to androgens is a situation in itself almost impossible to envision, since, apart from identical twins, the rest of the hormonal and nutritional milieu may be quite different. The fact that the spatial ability of adult men can vary with the changing testosterone levels across different seasons and times of day also clearly tells us that biological systems are not immutable.

However, the changeability of biological processes and the fact that we cannot at this stage of knowledge specify exactly how in the nervous system they have their effect on cognition are not excuses for dismissing them as unimportant factors. Critics of the theory that sex hormones influence spatial ability may, for example, chip away at each study that bears on this issue. They may point out uncontrolled variables in one study or may offer plausible alternative explanations in another study. Such critics often use the word *prove*, suggesting that a particular study, because of some limitation (and no study on human beings can ever be perfect), does not prove a hypothesis. Quite true, no one study is likely to sufficiently support a hypothesis to the point where we accept it wholly. Scientists do not expect to prove a position, they expect either to disprove it or to find sufficient and wide-ranging evidence for it, so that it becomes more and more plausible and alternative explanations become less and less likely. Human behavioral science, especially, must operate by looking at the cumulative evidence, not just at one study.

Another important criterion for accepting one hypothesis as more plausible than another, is how well the hypothesis fits with facts in other related fields of science, such as physiology, neuroscience, or evolutionary biology. If two hypotheses both appear able to account for substantial parts of the data, but one is also consistent with other bodies of pertinent facts, we are more likely to accept the explanation that has a broader base of support.

For example, research suggests that men and women differ in the degree to which they are distressed by sexual, as compared to emotional infidelity in their partners (Buss et al. 1996). Men, on average, are more affected by evidence of sexual infidelity and women more by emotional infidelity. Both socialization and sociobiological explanations of these facts have been proposed. The former stress the societal influences on different attitudes in men and women; the latter employ evolutionary concepts. On balance, because the evolutionary explanations are more broad-based, involving reference to the differing certainties of maternity and paternity (a woman always knows she is the parent) and the differing degree of parental investment between males and females (women invest more in their offspring), we would be inclined to accept the evolutionary explanation over the socialization one. Ultimately, of course, the deciding criterion is evidence.

Similarly, in the field of ability differences, the large sex difference in throwing accuracy has been attributed by some to the differing sports histories of men and women. Others, myself included, have suggested that this sex difference probably arises in some way from the division of labor between men and women over our long evolutionary history, during which men were the hunters and defenders. Even apart from the fact that the sex difference survives statistical correction for sports history, we would be inclined to give greater weight to the evolutionary explanation, because it fits better with knowledge of men's and women's different roles in those societies relatively unaffected by modern technology. We also have comparative data suggesting that even in a related primate, the chimpanzee, males throw objects much more frequently than females do.

We have mentioned that a common fallacy in research on human individual differences, including sex differences, is the tendency to impute such outcomes to different experiences. While we would not deny that experience contributes something to individual differences, we must be cautious in inferring that the experience *determines* the abilities. It may be the other way around. That is, we all choose our activities to some extent, and we generally tend to choose those that we are good at, with the result that we also gain more experience with those activities. So it isn't necessarily true that men are better at certain spatiomotor tasks because they have had experience at sports. Rather, they may choose certain sports because they have the appropriate abilities. This need not be consciously done—the positive reinforcement we get from doing something well, and the praise that ensues, may simply make such activities more attractive and more likely to occur. This phenomenon, whereby people end up in activities or occupations in a nonrandom or self-directed way, is called *self-selection*.

Different Criteria for Research on Sex Differences?

Some feminist critics have argued that cognitive and brain differences between men and women should be ignored, because there is a great deal of overlap between the two groups (Fausto-Sterling 1992: 251, Favreau 1993). It is certainly true that, in the larger context of comparison with other species, the similarities between men and women far outweigh the differences. However, if we were to adopt the criterion of *no overlap* between groups as a requirement for accepting a difference, we would find almost no behavioral data in any field to be acceptable. For example, if we were studying the effects of aging on memory, there would always be overlap in the scores of older and younger people. Yet we infer with some confidence that memory is, on average, not as good in the elderly. Even factors that have dramatic effects, such as damage to the brain, will often show a fair amount of overlap in the performance of those with and without brain damage. Why should sex differences be treated differently from other kinds of data?

In answer, it has been suggested that the more serious the consequences of accepting a hypothesis, the higher the level of supporting evidence should be before we accept it (Foss 1996). By "serious consequence" is presumably meant some possible application of a finding. There are strong reasons why such an approach is dangerous. First, it is difficult to think of any finding in behavioral science that will have absolutely no application in the larger world. The history of science makes it clear that it is impossible to predict which basic research will generate "useful" applications. Even in labs devoted to esoteric studies in cognitive psychology, a finding that recognition or recall of certain stimuli is better under one condition of presentation than another might well have application in education, or in some field of human engineering. It might, for example, suggest certain optimal ways of arranging work stations.

Moreover, if by application we mean *social* application, such an approach would require that a researcher decide whether his or her study has some *social consequence*, a term that has different meanings to different people. Are we then to have a research commissariat to decide whether a particular finding has sufficient social consequence to warrant a different level of evidence? Is the researcher then expected to apply a different statistical test or a differential weight of evidence, depending on whether the answer to the question of ultimate social importance is yes or no? To some extent, unfortunately, this already happens in the editorial screening of papers submitted to journals. I know of more than one occasion when a paper (not my own) on a controversial topic was either rejected on that basis or subjected to more intense scrutiny than would operate for other subjects.

This is objectionable and absurd. The rules of evidence and the stringency of statistical evaluation must be the same for all findings. Facts are neutral. We can't allow ourselves to get into a situation in which we say, "People won't like this finding, so acceptance must be at a more stringent level, whereas this other finding, which people will approve of, can be accepted more readily"! Or, "This is a finding that won't upset anyone, so I'm willing to generalize from it, but this other finding may be unpopular, so I need more evidence to support it before reporting it." Fortunately, science is a self-correcting discipline, with each successive finding modifying or refining earlier ideas. So even though as fallible human beings we sometimes make mistakes of inference, the truth ultimately will out.

Further Reading

Buss D.M., Larsen R.J. & Westen D. (1996) Sex differences in jealousy. *Psychological Science*, 7, 373–375.

Caplan P.J. & Caplan J.B. (1994) *Thinking critically about research on sex and gender*. New York: HarperCollins.

Fausto-Sterling A. (1992) *Myths of gender*. New York: Basic Books. (An avowedly feminist writer, Fausto-Sterling talks about the necessity for higher standards of "proof" for sex differences on page 11; and about the extent of overlap between the sexes as a basis for ignoring most sex differences, on page 251.)

Favreau O.E. (1993) Do the Ns justify the means? Null hypothesis testing applied to sex and other differences. *Canadian Psychology, 34*, 64–77.

Foss J.E. (1996) Is there a natural sexual inequality of intellect? A reply to Kimura. *Hypatia, 11*, 24–46.

Hilborn K.H.W. (1996) *The quest for "equality."* Toronto: C-FAR.

Shepard R.N. (1987) Evolution of a mesh between principles of the mind and regularities of the world. In J. Dupre (Ed.), *The latest on the best: essays on evolution and optimality*. Cambridge Mass: MIT Press, pp. 251-275.

2

Our Evolutionary Legacy

The difference between men and women is to many people one of the most intriguing of all human phenomena. Books, movies, television—in fact almost every aspect of our lives—reflect our fascination with what makes men and women different. We take it as given that there are two sexes in the world and that this division is preordained from conception. It is impossible to ignore the salient physical differences that we see in size, strength, distribution of hair, genital and breast shape, and so on.

For most of human existence it has probably also been taken for granted that differences in behavior are built in and that it is *natural* for men and women to diverge in aggression, energy, dominance, assertiveness, and problem solving. Only in very recent times has this view been challenged. In the last few decades, social concepts driven initially by women's enlarged roles during industrial expansion and large-scale modern wars—and by egalitarian philosophies—have shifted opinion to the opposite, extreme position: that there are no intellectual or personality differences between men and women that cannot be explained by different childrearing practices, that is, by socialization.

We know that, on average, men are superior to women on a variety of spatial skills, though women are better at some tasks requiring memory for the location of objects. Men also perform better on tests of mathematical reasoning, though women tend to be better at calculation. Contrary to popular opinion, adult women are not superior on all or most verbal tasks but primarily excel at memory for verbal material and at tasks of verbal fluency on which, for example, words must be generated with constraints on the beginning letter. Women also do better than men at tasks of perceptual speed calling for the rapid matching of visual items.

On motor skills, men are very much better at targeting tasks, such as throwing a missile accurately, whereas women are better at small-amplitude, fine motor skills. These and other sex differences in abilities will be reviewed in detail in later chapters.

People who do research on sex differences (we will use the biological term *sex* to refer to differences between males and females) are sometimes asked, "Why are you so interested in these differences? After all, men and women are alike in so many ways." For most of us the answer is, because they are there. But another important reason is that discovering the mechanisms for sex differences often helps us understand differences not only between men and women but between individuals of the same sex as well. So if we find, for example, that on average there is a certain brain difference between men and women, then we can investigate whether persons with one kind of brain pattern, whether men or women, also have cognitive or other characteristics that would be predicted by this feature.

As an example, let's assume that some of the connections between the hemispheres, the *commissures*, are more developed in women than in men. If we were to establish that larger commissures account for a particular female cognitive advantage (say, for the purposes of argument, their better verbal memory), then we could ask whether men with larger commissures also have better verbal memory than men with smaller commissures. In other words, we would have found a way to learn something about how the brain mediates certain behavioral traits that could apply to both men and women. Similar principles apply to studying the relations between sex-hormone levels and cognitive function.

To understand the differences that now appear between the sexes, we need to go beyond the study of men and women in a contemporary setting. If we consider how men and women differ from each other only in terms of modern-life situations, we will probably overlook some important aspects of human behavior. The human brain is organized essentially like that of our ancestors of fifty thousand and more years ago. In fact, our brains are the products of millions of years of evolution, and we clearly did not undergo natural selection for reading or for operating computers. So if we are to gain a better understanding of human behavior, including cognitive skills ,we must ask what the environment and the social structure was like over the long period in which our brain characteristics evolved.

Evolutionary explanations for the differences that now exist between men and women depend on some form of *natural selection*, in which the environment "selects" those traits of individuals that enhance survival (Darwin 1859, 1872). Thus traits that make it more likely that an individual will survive to reproductive age will thereby also make it more likely that the trait will be transmitted to the offspring. Applied to sex differences in behavior, this kind of explanation invokes not only a difference in reproductive roles but also other divergences in activity between the sexes over our long history as hominids. Such a division of labor suggests that the environment might have selected for somewhat different skills in males and females.

For much of our history, humans seem to have lived in a seminomadic society in which the gathering of plant foods was supplemented by scavenging and/or by hunting live animals. Later hominids apparently clustered in relatively small, often related groups. The subsequent shorter period of agricultural settlements was not radically different in style from the earlier stages and probably did not significantly alter the division of labor between men and women.

A variant of natural selection, called *sexual selection*, is said to operate when there is competition of males for females. Sometimes this results when females prefer, or select, males for certain characteristics that are, therefore, more likely to be passed on to the offspring. For example, the human male's generally larger size might be present in part because it was selected for by females. Note that the term *selection* does not imply a purposive selection on the part of individuals. It means only that those females who chose larger males as mates may have enhanced the chances that their (and the males') offspring would survive, compared to the offspring of smaller males. The preference for larger males would thus be passed on as a female trait.

Another type of sexual selection refers to characteristics resulting from male-to-male competition. For example, early hominid males who covered larger territories would have been more likely to encounter more females, have more mating opportunities, and thus have more reproductive success. Larger territories are related to better spatial ability in the males of certain nonhuman mammals, (Gaulin and Hoffman 1987) and it is conceivable that similar mechanisms operated in hominids at some point in our history.

It has been estimated that the largest hunter–gatherer group consisted of only about a hundred and fifty people and that, although other such groups would be encountered, prolonged contact would not be common. Imagine living your life knowing and sharing the background of almost everyone you deal with on a daily basis. Most of us now live in a world in which we daily encounter people we have never met before and about whom we know nothing. Our lives have changed drastically in the last few hundred years, but we are still equipped only with the genetic heritage appropriate to a very different society. It should not surprise us if we have problems dealing with these social changes.

The same may be said about relations between men and women. In the society in which we evolved, men and women were necessarily engaged in a cooperative effort—to produce children and to feed and shelter them to adulthood, when they in turn could continue the process of reproduction. Competition between man and woman, husband and wife, would not have been adaptive in an environment so harsh that their lives were almost wholly taken up with survival as a family within a limited social group. Because of the male's greater physical strength and his role as scavenger, hunter, and defender, there would generally have been a fairly stable arrangement, with the man in the dominant role. This is not to suggest that there were no tensions within the traditional family, nor that women had no input into family decisions—we know from observing remaining technologically simple societies today that women do influence many life decisions—but clearly males had the decisive voice (Goldberg 1993).

The activities that early men and women engaged in were also quite different, and have remained different in existing simple societies. Men were active in manufacturing tools, weapons, and transport devices. They were engaged in scavenging and in hunting small and large game, often traveling far from their home base. They were also responsible for defending the group against predators and enemies. Women contributed by gathering food near the home, preparing food and food-related utensils, making clothing, and caring for the home. The other major difference between men and women was in the care of infants, which was and remains almost exclusively the prerogative of women. There is no society in which men are the chief caregivers to small children.

This division of labor, as we said, might put different selection pressures on men and women, men most probably being selected for long-distance navigation—which requires the ability to recognize a scene from various orientations—and for accurate targeting. It has also been suggested that, to the extent that men were primarily responsible for making tools—because of their greater strength—some spatial skills may have evolved in relation to the necessity for symmetry in toolmaking (Wynn Tierson, and Palmer, 1996). Women, in contrast, might be selected for fine motor skills, short-range navigation using landmarks, and efficient perceptual discriminations. The latter would enable them to detect small changes, such as those in a child's face, or slight displacements in the home that might signal an intruder.

Another, less likely possibility we should keep in mind is that cognitive differences between men and women might be merely the by-products of some other sex difference important to survival. For example, it may be that the same male hormonal makeup that provided the optimal mechanism for the stamina or the independence to wander far from home in search of a mate or sustenance for one's family also fortuitously resulted in a high level of spatial ability, without that ability itself necessarily being selected for. Other possible mechanisms may exist.

Whatever the ultimate explanation for these differences between the sexes, they appear to have been with us since time immemorial and have left a behavioral legacy that is likely to survive for many generations to come. Even though our lives are very different from those of our ancestors, in fact very different from those of even a few generations ago, our human heritage remains essentially the same as that of preliterate hunter–gatherer and small-farming societies prevalent until fairly recently. In short, too few generations have elapsed for significant evolutionary changes to have occurred. Keeping this evolutionary framework in mind as we discuss the cognitive differences between the sexes will help us reach a better understanding of the fundamental nature of these differences.

Summary

To better comprehend the differences in behavior that we see between men and women, we need to look beyond modern times to the periods in which our brain characteristics evolved. We have obviously not undergone natural selection for the ability to read or operate computers, since these activities have a very recent history. Some other cognitive skills must have been their precursors. Men and women have a very long evolutionary history of division of labor, with men more actively involved in hunting or scavenging, which would take them farther from their home base. They also appear to have been better at throwing projectiles of various kinds. Early women, in contrast, stayed nearer the settlement and contributed to the food supply primarily by gathering. Their most crucial contribution would have been the care of infants and small children. It is likely that the average difference between the sexes in cognitive pattern and in motor skills arose chiefly out of such complementary evolutionary histories.

Further Reading

Daly M. & Wilson M. (1983, 2nd edition) *Sex, evolution and behavior*. Boston: PWS Publishers. (These authors outline Darwin's theory of natural selection, discuss the special case of "sexual selection," and apply these principles to explain a number of human sex differences in behaviour.)

Gaulin S.J.C. & Hoffman H.A. (1987) Evolution and development of sex differences in spatial ability. In L.L. Betzig, M. Borgerhoff Mulder & P.W. Turke (Eds.), *Human reproductive behaviour: a Darwinian perspective*. Cambridge: Cambridge Univ. Press, pp. 129–152.

Goldberg S. (1993) *Why men rule*. Chicago: Open Court Publ. Co. (Goldberg suggests that there never has been [and never will be] a society in which women dominate.)

Wynn T.G., Tierson F.D. & Palmer C.T. (1996) Evolution of sex differences in spatial cognition. *Yearbook of Physical Anthropology, 39*, 11–42.

3

How Males and Females Become Different

In humans, the genetic makeup required for becoming a male is having an X and a Y chromosome on the 23rd pair of chromosomes, and for becoming a female, having two X chromosomes. It might seem that nothing else is required to produce the two sexes, but it turns out it's not that simple. XY persons do typically become males, and XX persons do generally become females, but the process, at least in the case of males, is not direct or inevitable.

Most of the differences between males and females are *secondary* consequences of the presence or absence of the Y chromosome. The Y chromosome, in the normal course of events, determines that testes (male gonads) rather than ovaries (female gonads) will form; the testes, in turn, help determine most of the other differences between the sexes.

Many of the details we know about sexual differentiation come from studies on rats and mice. Most animal species are said to be bipotential in terms of sex, that is, they initially have undifferentiated gonads that can become testes or ovaries. The early embryo's basic structure can become either male or female. So the critical first step in the production of a male is the formation of testes which produce the male sex hormones needed to finish the job, including among other things, forming the male genitals. The "testis-determining factor" has been assumed to be carried on the Y chromosome, but until recently its precise location and nature were unknown. Currently a strong candidate for testis determination is the Sry gene on the Y chromosome. Koopman (Koopman, Gubbay, Vivian, Goodfellow, and Lovell-Badge, 1991) has shown that transplanting the Sry gene into a female (XX) mouse embryo can result in formation of a male whose testes secrete male hormones. Such a mouse will copulate normally with female mice, but is sterile, that is, it produces no sperm.

If there are no male hormones, a female will form, and it appears that no special hormonal milieu is needed to yield a female. Males, however, are formed only when testosterone is produced by the testes, and when the tissue in the organism reacts to the testosterone or its derivatives. We can summarize the process of sexual differentiation by saying that the "default" or "basic" form in mammals is a female, and that the male might be considered a variation on the female. In the embryo, testes develop earlier than ovaries do, perhaps to overcome the natural tendency for a female to form.

Two sets of ducts, only one of which typically survives, are initially present in both male and female mammals. Wolffian ducts ultimately form male internal reproductive structures and the Müllerian ducts form female internal structures (figure 3.1). If testes are present, two things happen in the ducts as a result of two different substances produced by the testes—testosterone and Müllerian regression factor (MRF). Testosterone develops the Wolffian ducts and MRF causes the Müllerian ducts to dissolve. In females, who have ovaries, there is of course no MRF, so the Müllerian ducts are able to develop, but the Wolffian ducts do atrophy. Why the Wolffian ducts disappear in females is unclear, except that they do require testosterone to develop.

The next major step in making a male is formation of the external genitals, the penis and scrotum, the latter being the pouch which will contain the testes outside the body cavity later in life (figure 3.2). Testosterone is critical also for this step, but it works by being converted to a related compound, dihydrotestosterone (DHT). Conversion from T to DHT is achieved by an enzyme called 5-alpha-reductase, which is normally present in the genital tissue of both males and females; it is only effective when sufficient T is available, that is, in males. If for some reason the quantity of 5-alpha-reductase is insufficient or the enzyme is absent, the external genitals look female, even though there are testes inside the abdomen, and even though the Wolffian ducts are developed and the Müllerian ducts have regressed. As you can see, there are several stages of development into a male when variation from the "norm" can occur,

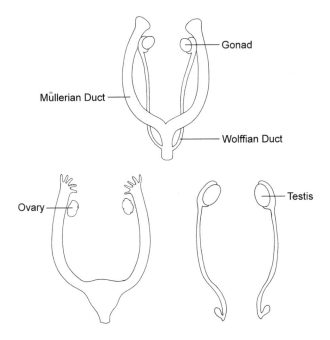

Figure 3.1
(Top) The undifferentiated gonad and two sets of ducts (Müllerian-female; Wolffian-male). (Bottom) The gonads ultimately become ovaries (female) or testes (male), with differentiation of ducts into Fallopian tubes and uterus (left), or vas deferens and seminal vesicles (right).

whereas so far as we know at present, hormonal support is not critical in producing the genital structures of a female.

It is a reasonable assumption that all mammals have roughly similar mechanisms of sexual differentiation, and what facts we have support the idea that human sex is determined in a fashion parallel to that of the rodent. Some of this evidence comes from human sexual anomalies. For example, some genetic males (XY) are born without sensitivity to androgens, the group of hormones which includes testosterone, DHT, androstenedione, and others that have masculinizing effects. The body cells of such people have no androgen "receptors," small structures within the cell that respond to the hormones to produce their effects. These androgen-insensitive individuals form testes in the usual way (though they remain inside the abdominal cavity), and the testes produce testosterone,

Undifferentiated

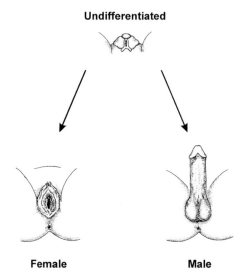

Female   Male

Figure 3.2
(Top) Undifferentiated external genitals. (Bottom) These differentiate into female (left) or male (right) genitals. (After Nelson, 1995. Reprinted by permission from Sinauer Associates Inc.)

but the body tissues do not respond. As a consequence, the male or Wolffian ducts don't develop, and the female or Müllerian ducts usually disappear because the testes produce effective quantities of MRF. Because the genital tissue is insensitive to T and DHT, the scrotum and penis do not develop.

These genetic males therefore look like females (figure 3.3) and are only discovered to be males at puberty, when they fail to menstruate. In fact they are typically quite curvaceous females, although, because of the androgen insensitivity, they have sparse pubic hair. Breasts form at the usual time, because the testes also produce some estrogen, and breast formation is related to the ratio of estrogen to effective testosterone in the tissue.

Another interesting developmental anomaly, discovered some time ago in the Dominican Republic, confirms the role of DHT in the formation of external genitals in human males. These XY individuals were born looking externally like girls, and were raised as girls. At puberty, how-

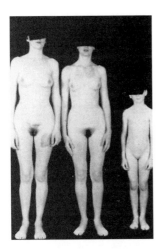

Figure 3.3
XY siblings with insensitivity to androgens and a female phenotype. Breasts are
well developed but pubic hair is scanty. (Reprinted by generous permission of Dr.
Charmian Quigley; originally published in Quigley et al., 1995.)

ever, male genitals began to form and the testes descended into a scrotum.
These males had a genetic deficiency in 5-alpha-reductase, the enzyme
that converts testosterone to dihydrotestosterone. As a result, although
they had functional internal testes, and developed Wolffian ducts, the
penis and scrotum did not develop. At puberty, however, when the testes
produced larger amounts of testosterone, even partial conversion to DHT
was apparently sufficient to masculinize the external genitals (Imperato-
McGinley, Guerrero, Gautier, and Peterson, 1974). Nearly all of these
males seem to have adapted well to the change in sex, most have married,
but to date none has been known to produce offspring.

Finally, to make the story in humans even more convincing, there are
the cases of what is called congenital adrenal hyperplasia (CAH). These
are individuals (male and female) who have been exposed to an excess of
androgens from their adrenal glands. The adrenals produce some androgens, notably androstenedione. Because these people are deficient in an
important enzyme that converts other adrenal substances to cortisol, their
brains send out signals to the adrenals to pour out more hormones. As a
result, the adrenal glands produce more androgens as well. In girls, the

increased androgen can have a masculinizing effect, and some of them are born with partially "virilized" or male genitals. This can be corrected by surgery, and the hormone production can be stopped by medications begun shortly after birth.

All these cases illustrate the powerful masculinizing effect of androgens in humans. We'll discuss them further when we consider the hormonal source of behavioral differences between human males and females in chapter 9.

Although we tend to speak of androgens as male hormones, and estrogens as female hormones, males and females both produce both types of hormones. The ovaries initially produce androgens, most of which are quickly converted in the ovary to estrogens. This conversion is done by a process called aromatization, which requires the presence of an enzyme called aromatase. The testes, in addition to producing testosterone, also convert some testosterone to estrogen. To further complicate the picture, as we just mentioned, the adrenal glands in both sexes produce androgens. Finally, the ovaries also produce a hormone called progesterone which is important during pregnancy.

So far we have been discussing the obvious structural differences between males and females—internal and external genitals, and breast formation. For males and females to adopt differing complementary roles in sexual behavior and reproduction, their brains must also somehow be made to work differently. Again, we can use other mammalian species as models to find out how this happens. In rodents, the typical sexual behavior involves, on the part of the female, certain inviting movements such as ear wiggling and hopping, as well as downward arching of the back (lordosis) and moving the tail aside, to allow the penis to enter the vagina. The male must have in his repertoire mounting behavior, in which he climbs partially onto the female's back and holds her with the forepaws, as well as intromission (placing the penis into the vaginal canal), thrusting movements, and finally ejaculation, the deposit of semen.

As with structural sexual differentiation, behavioral or brain sexual differentiation appears to depend, for the male, on the presence of sex hormones early in life. These early effects of sex hormones, which have lifelong irreversible effects on behavior, are called *organizational effects* (See Goy and McEwen, 1980). In the absence of sex hormones before and immediately after birth, the female pattern develops. We have come to know about this through a number of studies in which the hormonal state of an animal has been altered either before or just after birth. As it happens, the rodent brain remains sensitive to the effects of sex hormones for a few days immediately after birth, when the genital structures are already formed. This means that we can change the behavior so that it no longer corresponds, as an adult, to the structural or genital sex.

One common way of doing this is by castration (removing the testes but leaving the penis intact), thus stopping or significantly reducing the flow of androgens to the brain. If this is done to a rat in the first few days of life, then when the animal is full grown it will, with some priming from female sex hormones (called an *activational* effect), display *female* sexual behavior, such as lordosis, but little or no male sexual behavior. An adult male rat not castrated at birth will not show female behavior when given the same kind of hormonal priming, so the early exposure to androgens must somehow prevent it.

Removing the ovaries from a female rat right after birth does not affect either her adult sexual behavior or maternal behavior, in parallel with the way female genital structures differentiate. Of course, since without ovaries she cannot produce young, the maternal behavior has to be tested with another mother's litter. The general pattern seems to be that ovarian hormones are not essential for female brain organization, which occurs without the influence of sex hormones. However, some have argued that either the female's own ovarian hormones or her mother's hormones prenatally provide a low level of estrogen which is necessary to complete the "feminization" of the female brain (Dohler et al., 1984). In other words, they believe that female behavioral characteristics do not develop fully in the *absence* of sex hormones. This is currently an unresolved issue.

In the rodent, researchers have identified two fairly independent processes in the development of male sexual behavior. One is *masculinization*, the organization of such male behaviors as mounting, intromission, etc. The other, called *defeminization*, refers to the inhibition of female behaviors like lordosis, which will occur if not actively suppressed. Obviously both masculinization and defeminization must happen if normal male behavior is to occur. McEwen (1987) has suggested that defeminization occurs primarily after birth through the process of changing testosterone (paradoxically) to estrogen, through aromatization. So defeminization depends on the action of estrogen on estrogen receptors in the brain. Masculinization is thought to depend on the same route, plus the conversion of testosterone to DHT, via 5-alpha-reductase, and the consequent interaction of DHT with androgen receptors in the brain. The reader will recall that DHT was also essential for the formation of external male genitals. In primates, such as monkeys and perhaps humans, the testosterone-to-estrogen conversion may play a less important role, and the androgens a more salient one.

We know what we do about these processes through the use of several other methods, besides castration, of changing the animal's hormonal environment. These include administering sex hormones (for example, androgens or estrogens) to females right after birth; administering anti-androgens, such as flutamide, substances that block the effect of androgens, usually by occupying the receptors the androgens would affect; administering anti-estrogens such as tamoxifen; and employing compounds that block the conversion (aromatization) of testosterone to estrogen.

One puzzle that arises is why the female brain, which we would expect to be bombarded by the estrogen produced by the ovaries, is not also defeminized and partially masculinized by it. The tentative answer has been that in females the estrogen is captured in the blood stream by a substance called alpha-fetoprotein, which keeps estrogen from entering the brain cells. This substance is present in infants of both sexes, but since it does not bind to androgens, has no effect on males.

The fact that sexual behavior in rodents and primates can be radically altered by early exposure to sex hormones has raised the possibility that variation in exposure to hormones might be the basis for variation in sexual orientation in humans. One objection to this idea is that the hormones influence the likelihood that certain behaviors (for example, lordosis or mounting) will occur; whereas it is not necessarily particular *behaviors* which differentiate heterosexual and homosexual individuals, but a preference for the type of partner—same-sex or opposite-sex. Recent research by Brand and co-workers, however, has suggested that early hormonal manipulation in rats can also alter adult partner preference, making it somewhat more likely that sexual orientation in humans could result from a parallel mechanism (Brand, Kroonen, Mos, and Slob, 1991; Brand and Slob, 1991). The fact that girls with CAH, who have early over-exposure to androgens, tend to have a higher incidence of homosexual fantasy and preference than their unaffected sisters (Dittman, Kappes and Kappes, 1992) supports such a position. Of course, these findings do not rule out other contributing factors.

The importance of early organizational factors in influencing the life-long pattern of humans is also suggested in a recent review by Diamond and Sigmundson (1997) of cases in which the penis has been damaged shortly after birth. Because it is easier to construct a vagina than a penis, the common solution in such cases used to be to remove the testes as well, and attempt to rear the child as a girl. Diamond gives a detailed account of one boy whose penis was accidentally burnt off during surgery, at the age of eight months. At about one year of age his testicles were removed, and a vagina was later constructed. The apparent success with which he adopted a girl's role, reported much earlier by Money and Ehrhardt (1972), was widely accepted as evidence that human males and females are psychologically undifferentiated at birth.

Longer-term followup of this case, however, told quite a different story. Even in childhood this person showed play patterns and toy preferences more typical of boys than of girls. His walk and physique were reminiscent of males and resulted in a great deal of teasing from other children. He even tried to stand up to urinate! By the age of eight or nine years, he felt strongly that he was a boy. He rebelled at taking the estrogen prescribed at age twelve to induce breast formation, and finally at fourteen decided to live as a male. Only then did the parents reveal his early history, which he learned with great relief. He subsequently underwent breast removal surgery and had a penis constructed. Eventually he married a woman with two children, whom he adopted. He never had any sexual interest in males.

Several other cases in the literature have apparently run a similar course. If it is found to be generally true that such individuals prefer a male role despite an inadequate penis and being reared as girls, this would of course suggest that in humans also, as well as rodents, some aspects of behavioral masculinization are complete at birth or within a short period thereafter.

The masculinizing influence of sex hormones is not limited to reproductive behavior. In fact, it appears to operate for all behaviors so far studied that are sexually dimorphic—that is, in which males and females differ. For example, juvenile male rodents as well as monkeys show a high level of "rough-and-tumble" play, or play-fighting. This consists of boisterous activity in which there is a great deal of body contact, though the juveniles do not harm each other. Juvenile females normally show very little of this behavior, but at the same ages, female monkeys appear to spend a fair amount of time in infant-carrying behavior, within the limits permitted by the mother (Meaney, Lozos, and Stewart, 1990). In most human societies too, boys are reported to show a higher level of rough-and-tumble play than girls do. This is not merely a difference in activity level (in which boys and girls are more equivalent), but in a preponderance of rough-housing, characterized by close physical contact.

Michael Meaney (Meaney and McEwen, 1986) has worked out the probable brain and hormonal mechanisms in rodents for the organization of this play-fighting activity in rodents. It appears to depend on testosterone-to-DHT conversion, with DHT having its effect primarily on androgen receptors in a brain structure called the amygdala. The amygdala is known to be important in the expression of fear and aggression. If male rats are deprived of androgens, or female rats are exposed to them shortly after birth, as juveniles they will show sex-atypical behavior. The deprived males show less, and treated females more, rough-and-tumble play.

There may be a parallel mechanism in humans, since girls with CAH are reportedly more "tomboyish" than unaffected girls. They also are more active in sports involving rough body contact (Hampson, Rovet, and Altmann, 1995). Equally interesting is the finding that CAH girls have toy preferences that are strikingly similar to boys. It is well established that boys and girls differ in some toy preferences, with most boys preferring to play with vehicles and construction toys, and most girls preferring dolls or stuffed animals. Many people (at least until they have children of their own) believe that these preferences are taught by parents and other adults. However, CAH girls show a strong preference for "boys'" toys, and there is every reason to believe that the parents of CAH girls are at least as likely to encourage them to be feminine, and thus to play with girls' toys, as other parents are. Despite this probable socializing influence, the CAH girls play with dolls less, and with vehicles more, than normal girls (Berenbaum and Hines, 1992). There is also some evidence that CAH girls tend to have less interest in real infants than unaffected girls do, and that they don't differ from boys in this respect (Leveroni and Berenbaum, 1998). So there is a strong probability that prenatal exposure to hormones is the basis for the difference normally seen between boys and girls in toy and baby-tending preferences. (We discuss the contribution of such androgenic influences in CAH cases to spatial ability in chapter 9.)

One of the important features of the early organizing effect of sex hormones on behavior is that not all behaviors are susceptible to these influences at the same time. Recall that one of the important components of masculine sexual behavior in rats is mounting onto the partner's back. Administering testosterone to mothers prenatally would result in exposure of the fetal brain to androgens, and would therefore be expected to increase mounting behavior in the female offspring when they are adult. Goy has shown that, in monkeys, testosterone is most effective in increasing mounting in the daughters if it is administered early in the mother's pregnancy (Goy, Bercovitch, and McBrair, 1988). In these early-treated females, rough-and-tumble play is only slightly increased. However, testosterone administered later in gestation has a minimal effect on the daughters' mounting behavior, but greatly increases the play-fighting.

This must mean that the nervous system mechanisms for mounting and for rough-and-tumble play develop at different times before birth. We have already mentioned that masculinization and defeminization of sexual behavior in the male rat also occur at somewhat different times. These findings are important because they open up the possibility that prenatal hormonal variation that is restricted in time can affect some aspects of behavioral masculinization but leave others unaffected. Such phenomena may be relevant, for example, to human homosexuality, where gender identification and many other behaviors are sex-typical, but partner preference is not.

Summary

Most of the differences between male and female mammals are a secondary consequence of the presence or absence of the Y chromosome. Typically, the Y chromosome results in formation of male gonads, testes, which secrete the androgens that guide the formation of male genitalia, and of male-typical behavior. In the absence of effective androgens, a female develops.

Anomalies of human hormonal development suggest that the human situation is similar to that of other mammals. Thus XY individuals without functional androgen receptors look and act like females; whereas XX individuals with excess early exposure to androgens may be born with virilized genitals and show some male-typical behaviors later in life.

There is evidence that the early sensitive time periods for masculinization of different behaviors, such as mounting and rough-and-tumble play, may be different. This fact might be relevant to sexual orientation, suggesting how homosexually oriented persons could be sex-atypical in partner preference, but nevertheless show sex-typical gender identity.

Further Reading

Berenbaum S.A. & Hines M. (1992) Early androgens are related to sex-typed toy preferences. *Psychological Science*, 3, 203–206.

Brand T., Kroonen J., Mos J. & Slob A.K. (1991) Adult partner preference and sexual behavior of male rats affected by perinatal endocrine manipulations. *Hormones & Behavior*, 25, 323–341.

Brand T. & Slob A.K. (1991) On the organization of partner preference behavior in female Wistar rats. *Physiology & Behavior*, 49, 549–555.

Diamond M. & Sigmundson K. (1997) Sex reassignment at birth. *Archives of Pediatric & Adolescent Medicine*, 151, 298–304.

Dittman R.W., Kappes M.E. & Kappes M.H. (1992) Sexual behavior in adolescent and adult females with congenital adrenal hyperplasia. *Psychoneuroendocrinology*, 17, 153–170.

Dohler K.D., Hancke J.L., Srivastava S.S., Hofmann C., Shryne J.E. & Gorski R.A. (1984) Participation of estrogens in female sexual differentiation of the brain; neuroanatomical, neuroendocrine and behavioral evidence. In G.J. DeVries, J.P.C. DeBruin, H.B.M. Uylings & M.A. Corner (Eds.), *Sex differences in the brain. Progress in Brain Research*, 61, Amsterdam: Elsevier, pp. 99–117.

Goy R.W., Bercovitch F.B. & McBrair M.C. (1988) Behavioral masculinization is independent of genital masculinization in prenatally androgenized female rhesus macaques. *Hormones & Behavior, 22,* 552–571.

Goy R.W. & McEwen B.S. (1980) *Sexual differentiation of the brain.* Cambridge: MIT Press. (Discusses the concepts of "organizational" and "activational" influences of hormones on behavior.)

Hampson E., Rovet J.F. & Altmann D. (1995) Sports participation and physical aggressiveness in children and young adults with congenital adrenal hyperplasia. Proceedings of the International Behavioral Development Symposium. *Biological basis of sexual orientation and sex-typical behavior.* Minot, North Dakota, p. 39.

Imperato-McGinley J., Guerrero L., Gautier T. & Peterson R.E. (1974) Steroid 5-alpha-reductase deficiency in man: an inherited form of male pseudohermaphroditism. *Science, 186,* 1213–1215.

Koopman P., Gubbay J., Vivian N., Goodfellow P. & Lovell-Badge R. (1991) Male development of chromosomally female mice transgenic for Sry. *Nature, 351,* 117–121.

Leveroni C.L. & Berenbaum S.A. (1998) Early androgen effects on interest in infants: evidence from children with congenital adrenal hyperplasia. *Developmental Neuropsychology, 14,* 321–340.

McEwen B.S. (1987) Observations on brain sexual differentiation: a biochemist's view. In J.M. Reinisch, L.A. Rosenblum & S.A. Sanders (Eds.), *Masculinity/femininity.* New York: Oxford Univ. Press, pp. 68–79.

Meaney M.J., Lozos E. & Stewart J. (1990) Infant carrying by nulliparous female vervet monkeys (Cercopithecus aethiops). *Journal of Comparative Psychology, 104,* 377–381.

Meaney M.J. & McEwen B.S. (1986) Testosterone implants into the amygdala during the neonatal period masculinize the social play of juvenile female rats. *Brain Research,* 398, 324–328.

Money J. & Ehrhardt A.A. (1972) *Man & woman. Boy & girl.* Baltimore: Johns Hopkins.

Nelson R.J. (1995) An introduction to behavioral endocrinology. Sunderland, Mass: Sinauer. (Includes an overview of the process of sexual differentiation.)

Quigley C.A., DeBellis A., Marschke K.B., El-Awady M.K., Wilson E.M. & French F.S. (1995) Androgen receptor defects: Historical, clinical and molecular perspectives. *Endocrine Reviews, 16,* 271–321.

4

Motor Skills

Most so-called "cognitive" tests that differentiate the sexes, and many of those we will talk about in this book, are administered in a paper-and-pencil format; that is, the problems are presented in printed form, preceded by instructions and by practice items. These tests typically have a time limit, usually of a kind that prevents most people from finishing all items. You may have had experience with tests of this kind, if you've taken aptitude tests or certain intelligence tests.

Particular tests are often chosen for research because they are relatively "pure," meaning that they have been shown to measure primarily one type of ability. They differ from real-life problem-solving in at least two important ways—most of the problems we encounter in everyday life engage several different abilities; and involve some kind of coordinated physical activity, other than just writing an answer. While it is important to know about the results from paper-and-pencil tests, if we look only at them, we may miss some of the other ways in which men and women differ in skills.

One of the largest, most reliable sex differences in ability that we know about involves an unalloyed real-world motor activity—accuracy in aiming objects at a target. The differences between adult men and women in throwing accuracy, or *targeting* as we shall call it, are as great as those seen on spatial rotation tasks, the other ability on which men and women differ most sharply. But should we consider targeting a problem-solving or cognitive task? Could it not be just a matter of strength or speed, consequently a by-product of men's greater muscle bulk or faster-responding muscle fibers? Or is it simply that men enjoy targeting games more than women do and so they have practiced a great deal more?

Plausible as all these suggestions seem, they probably are not the major explanation for this sex difference.

Harking back to our evolutionary account of how differences between men and women came about, one of the most valuable skills for early hominid hunters would have been the ability to strike a prey by throwing a rock or some other missile at it. Doing so requires the hunter to coordinate information about the target's precise location, direction, and speed, with the aiming action of the hands, arms, and indeed the whole body. Even with a stationary object, targeting requires significant skill, but when the object is a small moving animal, the prediction of location requires rapid spatial analysis and exquisite timing in directing the action of muscle groups. While strength is important in determining the speed of movements, the spatiomotor analysis is even more critical.

In existing hunter-gatherer societies, men are almost exclusively the sex involved in hunting, and there is reason to believe that this is and was universally true (Daly and Wilson, 1983; Murdock, 1965). It is interesting that chimpanzees also show a sharp sexual dimorphism, favoring males, in the incidence of throwing, whether aimed at a target or not (Goodall, 1986). Chimpanzees are not primarily carnivores, however, and don't hunt animals with missiles. Their accuracy in throwing is quite poor. It appears that for them, throwing is part of an aggressive display. Conceivably, human throwing might also have begun as a means of frightening off predators, and then evolved into a more directed mechanism for defence, as well as for hunting.

The sharp division of labor between men and women seen in targeting activities across all human societies might be expected to manifest itself in a sizable sex difference, and the difference in accuracy on a variety of targeting tasks is indeed large. On a dart-throwing task studied in our lab (figure 4.1), men were more accurate then women by at least a full standard deviation (effect size greater than 1.0) than were women. The same was true of an interception task (figure 4.2), where the subject was required only to bring his or her hand in contact with, but not actually catch, a pingpong ball flung from a launcher. In contrast, the same subjects showed much smaller effect sizes (of .5 or less) on the paper-and-pencil spatial tests (Watson and Kimura, 1991), some of which are described in chapter 5. Since these same men and women did not differ

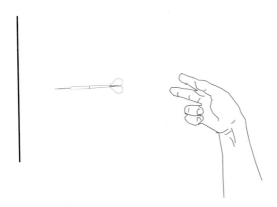

Figure 4.1
Example of a dart-throwing task. Men are, on average, much more accurate than women.

in their reaction time to a visual target, simple speed of reaction did not account for the more accurate interception.

The fact that neither reaction time, nor height, nor weight, accounted for the large sex difference on the interception task suggests that it requires rapid spatiomotor analysis and coordination not simply reducible to muscle characteristics. The finding that throwing and intercepting correlated minimally, if at all, with the paper-and-pencil spatial tasks also suggests that targeting represents a relatively separate ability; that is, whether a person is good at targeting seems to be unrelated to how well he or she performs tests requiring only mental manipulation of spatial information.

We are all aware that men predominate in most individual and team sports, many of which require accurate aiming of a puck, ball, or some other object. Although women now engage in sports activities to a much greater extent than they did a couple of generations ago, male and female competitions are nearly always held separately. This is because men clearly have the advantage.

Of course, the men in our study also engaged in sports activities involving targeting to a greater extent than the women did. However, when we evaluated the detailed sports history we had taken from all our subjects, we found that the effect of past participation in target-related sports accounted for a negligible portion of the difference between the

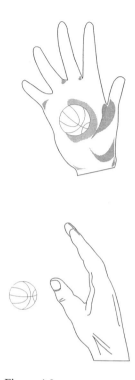

Figure 4.2
An interception task. The subject needs only to stop the ball with the hand, not catch it. Men are superior also on this task.

sexes (Watson and Kimura, 1991). Instead, it seems there is a basic difference between men's and women's targeting ability which is not reducible to differential experience. In any case, we would ask why it is that men are so much more likely to spontaneously take part in such target-directed activities.

Evidence that sex differences in throwing accuracy are not simply a consequence of differences in strength or physique comes from a study of homosexual subjects. In this study, we employed a vertically hung carpet marked out in squares around a central target. Subjects attempted to hit the target with a velcro-covered ball which stuck to the carpet (figure 4.3) (Hall and Kimura, 1995). Homosexual men were on average significantly less accurate than heterosexual men on this targeting task, and in fact were not significantly better than heterosexual women. Yet the homosex-

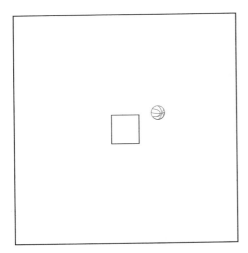

Figure 4.3
Another version of a targeting task. A velcro-covered ball is thrown against a carpet, and sticks to it. A horizontal version of this task was used for young children.

ual men were, like most men, taller and stronger than the women, and were not distinguishable from heterosexual men in height or weight. Again, although there were differences in sports history between the two male groups, this experience did not account for the difference in targeting. We should also point out that the "gender identity" of the homosexual men was of course male, indicating that this is not a major determinant of targeting ability. On other paper-and-pencil spatial tasks on which men and women differ, differences between homosexual and heterosexual men are disputed, and are far less reliable than those found on targeting tasks (Gladue and Bailey, 1995; Sanders and Wright, 1997).

Male superiority on targeting appears very early in life, before boys and girls differ markedly in muscle bulk and strength, or have had much differential targeting experience. Diane Lunn (1987) and I investigated targeting ability in boys and girls between three and five years of age. We decided to have them use an underhanded throw to diminish a possible advantage from boys' different skeletomuscular structure. We also employed a horizontal target—a rug on the floor marked out in squares—to reduce the possible effects of differential experience in hitting a conventional upright target. The missile was again a velcro-covered ball, thrown to a central target on the rug. Boys were significantly more accurate than girls on this task, although on perceptual tasks, with lesser motor involvement, there were no differences.

In contrast to targeting, on certain *fine* motor tasks, women do better than men. Again, one might predict this on the basis of the tasks that women were predominantly engaged in in preliterate societies—gathering of small foods such as berries, making pottery, weaving, manufacturing thread and cordage, and so forth. The Purdue Pegboard, a standard test originally designed to select for factory jobs requiring manual skill, shows a consistent advantage for women (figure 4.4). On the simplest trials of this test, subjects pick up as many pegs as possible within a given time from a depression in the top of the board, and place them in appropriately sized holes in order along the board. In the more complex trials,

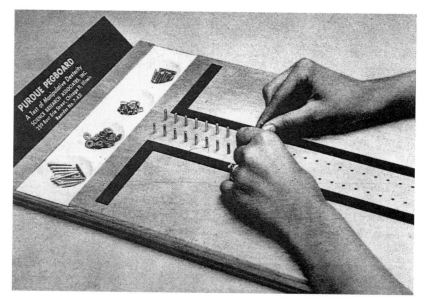

Figure 4.4
The Purdue Pegboard. Women excel on this task, which was developed to test applicants for manufacturing assembly jobs. (Reproduced by permission of Purdue Research Foundation, West Lafayette, Indiana 47907, who hold the copyright.)

they pick up a washer with the other hand, and slip it over the peg after they insert it. Some have argued that women's advantage on such fine motor tasks is accounted for by their smaller fingers; but while this may contribute to the sex difference in some studies (Peters, Servos, and Day, 1990), we have not found this to be the case in ours (Hall and Kimura, 1995; Nicholson and Kimura, 1996).

Other tests in our lab suggest that women have generally better control over their distal musculature (i.e., muscles farther from the body, as in the fingers) than men do; and that this is true even when they are not performing speeded tasks. For example, when subjects are required to bend a single finger or pairs of fingers at the middle joint, without allowing other fingers to move, women are better able to do this than men (Kimura and Vanderwolf, 1970). Similarly, young girls aged three to five reproduce hand postures—in which fingers must be placed in demonstrated configurations—more accurately than do boys of the same age (figure 4.5) (Ingram, 1975). Neither of these abilities should be influenced by finger size, and it is also difficult to see how such tasks would be influenced by socialization processes. Remember that at these same ages, boys are already more accurate at targeting.

There is some evidence to suggest that women may not only be superior in precise distal control, but also in the ability to coordinate several movements into a unit. For example, young girls are faster at touching each finger in succession against the thumb, but they show no advantage over boys at simply repeating the same finger-thumb movement over and over (Denckla, 1974). Adult women sometimes show similar advantages in performing a sequence of movements, for example, when several telegraph keys must be tapped in sequence by the fingers (Lomas and Kimura, 1976; Nicholson and Kimura, 1996). Men, however, tend to be faster at performing a single movement, such as tapping one key repeatedly with the same finger. The single tapping ability has been found to be related to strength.

The same pattern of sex differences may appear also in the speeded production of speech. Men tend to be faster at repeating a single syllable such as ba-ba-ba; whereas women tend to produce relatively more syllables when reproducing a sequence like ba-da-ga (Nicholson and Kimura, 1996).

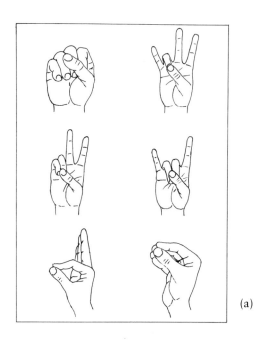

(a)

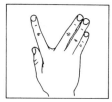

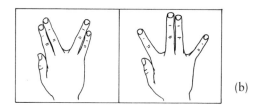

(b)

Figure 4.5
Hand Postures (a) and Finger Spacing (b) tasks. Girls copy such positions better than boys do.

Obviously women are not better at all coordinated movements, since males have the advantage in throwing accuracy. Perhaps women are better coordinated for small amplitude movements, and men for large amplitude movements; or women are better coordinated for movements within personal space, and men for movements directed at external space. There are still many unanswered questions about this distinction.

All individual variation in skills must be represented in the nervous system in some way. There have been many suggestions about how the brains of males and females differ, some of which are discussed in later chapters. One of the differences in organization that may be especially pertinent here is the degree to which complex motor control depends on the front (anterior) or back (posterior) parts of the brain. If men's motor coordination abilities emphasize directing movements at external space, visuospatial input would be crucial. Motor control systems employed in throwing would have to be meshed with visual systems, which are located at the posterior end of the brain. In fact, impairments of hand and arm movement control after posterior damage to the left hemisphere of the brain are more often seen in men than in women. These findings are discussed in more detail in chapter 11.

Summary

Men and women differ in the kinds of motor skills they excel at. Men are very much better than women at most kinds of targeting abilities, such as dart throwing, or intercepting a missile such as a ball. This advantage does not appear to be accounted for primarily by differences in physique, since homosexual men's targeting skills are not significantly better than women's. Young boys are more accurate than girls on similar tasks as early as age three. Although the sports history of men and women often differs, that factor does not account for the male superiority.

Women, in contrast, tend to be faster than men on a series of movements involving especially the fingers, sometimes described as fine motor skills. This is despite the fact that men tend to have faster movement times, for example, in repeating a finger tap over and over. So possibly it is the coordination of these movements into a pattern that takes place more quickly in women.

The female advantage on finger movement control can be seen even when speed is not a factor. Women are better able to bend individual fingers in isolation, and young girls can copy static hand postures more accurately, requiring precise placement of fingers, than can boys. Such motor tasks seem unlikely to be affected by hand size, which has sometimes been given as the explanation for women's superior fine movements.

Further Reading

Daly M. & Wilson M. (1983) *Sex, evolution and behavior*. Boston: Willard Grant Press. (On pp. 262–263, the authors list activities which are performed primarily by males or by females in 224 societies. To the "exclusively female" category we could add "Primary caregiver to infants.")

Denckla M.B. (1974) Development of motor co-ordination in normal children. *Developmental Medicine & Child Neurology*, 16, 729–741.

Gladue B.A. & Bailey J.M. (1995) Spatial ability, handedness, and human sexual orientation. *Psychoneuroendocrinology*, 20, 487–497.

Goodall J. (1986) *The chimpanzees of Gombe*. Cambridge: Harvard Univ. Press, pp. 549–559.

Hall J.A.Y. & Kimura D. (1995) Sexual orientation and performance on sexually dimorphic motor tasks. *Archives of Sexual Behavior*, 24, 395–407.

Ingram D. (1975) Motor asymmetries in young children. *Neuropsychologia*, 13, 95–102.

Kimura D. & Vanderwolf C.H. (1970) The relation between hand preference and the performance of individual finger movements by left and right hands. *Brain*, 93, 769–774.

Lomas J. & Kimura D. (1976) Intrahemispheric interaction between speaking and sequential manual activity. *Neuropsychologia*, 14, 23–33.

Lunn D. (1987) *Foot asymmetry and cognitive ability in young children*. Unpublished Master's thesis, Department of Psychology, University of Western Ontario, London, Canada.

Murdock G.P. (1965) *Culture and society*. Pittsburgh: Univ. Pittsburgh Press.

Nicholson K.G. & Kimura D. (1996) Sex differences for speech and manual skill. *Perceptual & Motor Skills*, 82, 3–13.

Peters M., Servos P. & Day R. (1990) Marked sex differences on a fine motor skill task disappear when finger size is used as a covariate. *Journal of Applied Psychology*, 75, 87–90.

Sanders G. & Wright M. (1997) Sexual orientation differences in cerebral asymmetry and in the performance of sexually dimorphic cognitive and motor tasks. *Archives of Sexual Behavior, 26*, 463–480.

Watson N.V. & Kimura D. (1991) Nontrivial sex differences in throwing and intercepting: relation to psychometrically-defined spatial functions. *Personality & Individual Differences, 12*, 375–385.

5
Spatial Abilities

Even the most skeptical egalitarian is usually willing to admit that there is an intrinsic difference between men and women on certain paper-and-pencil spatial tasks. The biggest and most reliable difference appears on what are often called "mental rotation" tests, where one is required to imagine what a given figure will look like in a new orientation (figure 5.1). The difference between the sexes is apparent on a variety of these "mental" or imaginary rotation tests, whether composed of familiar or unfamiliar figures, or whether rotation is depicted in two or three dimensions.

How might this sex difference have come about? As suggested in chapter 2, the division of labor in hominid societies would have put greater selection pressure on men to evolve long-range navigational skills, including, among other things, the capacity to recognize a scene from different angles or viewpoints, the kind of ability required for imaginal rotation. Figure 5.2 shows one test devised by Neil Watson and Gerry Stefanatos in our lab to examine this (Watson and Kimura, 1991). The task is to decide from which position, in degrees of the circle, one would see the grandfather figure in each depiction. As expected, men were much more often correct than women were, and the findings were the same whether the figure was a truck, tool, animal or, as in this case, a person.

Navigational skill might also call upon imaginal rotation ability in developing what is often called a *cognitive map*. When returning from a particular place, for example, we need to reverse the directions we took travelling to it. Or, if we do not come back along the identical route, we need to be able not only to reverse direction, but to combine that ability

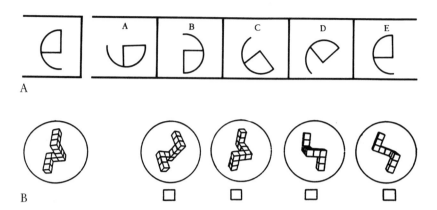

Figure 5.1
Two imaginal rotation tests: (a) An example from the PMA Spatial Relations test, a 2-dimensional test. The subject must pick all figures that could be the one on the left, rotated to a different orientation on the page. (Answers: B,D,E) (Reproduced by permission of the McGraw-Hill Companies Inc., from the 1962 Manual of the Primary Mental Abilities, Spatial Relations test.) (b) An example from Vandenberg and Kuse Mental Rotations test, the most popular "3-dimensional" test. The subject is instructed to pick the two figures that could be the same as the one on the left, when rotated in depth. (Answers: 1 and 3)(From Vandenberg and Kuse, 1978.)

with the capacity to put together parts of the route formerly seen piece-meal. In either case, we put demands on the ability to mentally rotate all or part of the route.

One alternative to the navigation hypothesis suggests that mental rotation may have become better developed in men due to their role in tool making. We suggested in the chapter on the evolution of skills that tool making, whether in stone or metal, was largely the prerogative of males. It has been proposed (Wynn, Tierson and Palmer, 1996) that in order to achieve the symmetry apparent in the tools made by later hominids, the ability to imaginally rotate the object would have been critical. One would have to assume that this ability was more essential for the making of stone tools than for symmetrical baskets (in which women partici-pated), perhaps because an error in making the stone tool could not be as easily undone.

Some have argued that the difference between men and women is especially apparent when rotation involves the third or depth dimension.

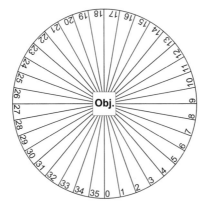

Subject

Figure 5.2
The grandpa figure from Watson and Stefanatos' Viewfinding test. The task is to decide from which position (0 to 35) the picture was taken. The picture on the left (a) is from the "0" position. Where is the picture on the right (b) taken from? (Answer: position 30) (From Watson and Kimura, 1991.)

Easy

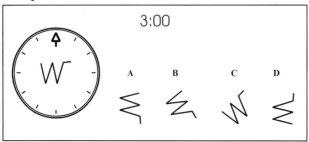

Hard

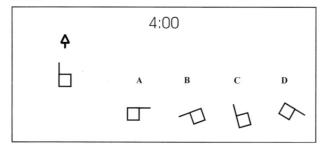

Figure 5.3
Collins' Two-Dimensional Clock test. In each case, the 12 o'clock position of the central figure is given on the left. The task is to decide how the central figure in the clock would look at the designated time, by picking one of the four choices. (Answers: [Easy] A; [Hard] D) (From Collins & Kimura, 1997.)

However, 3-D rotation tests are generally more difficult for everyone. To answer the question whether large sex differences appear only with 3-dimensional rotation, David Collins devised a very difficult 2-dimensional rotation test (figure 5.3). He found that the difference between men and women was at least as large on this test as on the classical 3-dimensional task (see figure 5.1b). So it may be that the more difficult the rotation task, the more easily we detect the sex difference. The 3-D task shown in figure 5.1b is the type most widely used in this kind of research, and it contains several elements, which makes it more complex.

Another interesting question is whether this rotational ability makes a significant contribution to any aspect of real life. It makes sense that it should, but is there any evidence that it does? One way to answer this is to see if imaginal rotation is significantly related to certain everyday skills, such as finding one's way. Ideally researchers would like to study how men and women differ in learning a route in the real world, but because this is often impractical, they typically substitute smaller-scale pictorial versions of the real thing.

A common finding from studies on traversing a route is that, when giving directions, women tend to use landmarks as referents, while men tend to use distance or cardinal directions (N,S,E,W). "Landmarks" refer to specific structures along the route, such as a building, bridge, or natural feature. A typical example using landmarks as direction markers would be "Go to the United Church and turn left. Turn right when you get to MacDonald's, that's Elm Street. You'll see the school at the end of

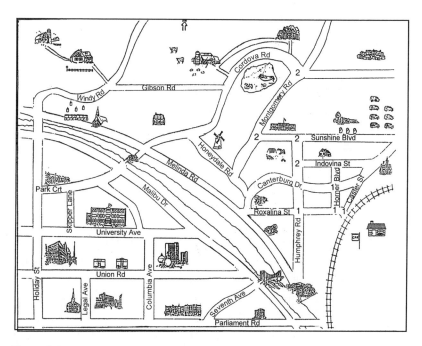

Figure 5.4
A reduced-size representation of a tabletop map on which subjects must learn a designated route. Men learn the route in fewer trials than women do, but women recall more of the landmarks along the way. (From Galea & Kimura, 1993.)

the block." Compare that with the use of directions, "Go north for half a mile, then turn east on Church Street for another half-mile, then north again on Elm Street. The school is at the end of the first block." The evidence suggests that men and women differ in their use of the two kinds of direction-giving, though of course not everyone behaves in a sex-typical fashion (Ward, Newcombe, and Overton, 1986).

We found similar effects when we asked young men and women to learn a new route (Galea and Kimura, 1993) through a tabletop map of the kind shown in figure 5.4. While the subject watched, we first traced a route through the map with a stylus that left no marks. Then we asked the subject to trace the same route from memory, with the experimenter correcting and counting errors as they occurred. We continued in this way until everyone had completed two errorless trials in a row. On average, men made fewer errors, took fewer trials to learn to the criterion, and so took less time altogether than did women. So to that extent, the sexes behaved as we might predict they would when learning a real-world route. The finding is consistent with reports that men have better map knowledge on average than women do (Beatty and Troster, 1987). An equally interesting finding from the study was the information about what was retained from the map after it had been learned. Men recalled correctly more details about directions and distances on the map, while women recalled more details about landmarks and street names.

The question we raised earlier, whether imaginal rotation ability is related to route learning, can be answered in the positive. Higher scores on a rotation task were associated (correlated) with better learning of the route, for both men and women. This apparently was not simply due to the fact that brighter people learned the route faster, and also got higher scores on the rotation test. Scores on a different test that also relates to overall intelligence, memory for objects presented (not the map items), were unrelated to map-learning scores. So the correlation between spatial rotation and map learning scores appears to indicate some specific ability common to both.

That idea is supported by another recent study that found a relation between performance on the classical rotation task (figure 5.1b) and performance on a computer-presented test simulating finding one's was

Figure 5.5
Silverman and Eals' Object Location Memory task: (a) presentation array (top) and (b) response array (bottom). The task is to identify the items that have changed location from the top to the bottom array. (Note that pairs of items have exchanged locations.) (Reproduced with permission from the authors, Silverman and Eals, 1992.)

through a labyrinth (Moffat, Hampson, and Hatzipantelis, 1998). The correlation between scores on the rotation and labyrinth tasks was about 0.60, whereas the correlation of the labyrinth with other kinds of spatial tests was lower, and with verbal tests lower still. It appears that some factor in imaginal rotation ability is a significant component of route learning, though it is by no means the only component. It might contribute even more to learning in a real-world route situation, but at present there is no evidence bearing on this question.

We generally speak of men being better at spatial tasks, but the term "spatial" has a variety of meanings. On one kind of spatial test, recalling the location of objects in an array, it appears that women may be better than men. Marion Eals and Irwin Silverman (1994) presented subjects with an array of line-drawings of familiar objects, then showed them a second array in which some pairs of the objects had exchanged locations (figure 5.5). The task was to identify which objects had been moved. Women were better than men at identifying the displaced objects. This remained true even when tested with objects that were relatively unfamiliar, or when they were nonsense shapes, so that names were less likely to be helpful. We have found similar results when we had subjects view an array of objects, and later gave them the objects to put back in their original positions.

The idea that these findings indicate better object location memory in women is reinforced by another recent study (McBurney, Gaulin, Devineni, and Adams, 1997), which made use of a commercial product called the Memory Game. Several matched pairs of cards with pictures of objects on them are placed facedown on the table, and the aim of the game is to turn them up in identical pairs. On each trial, the subject may turn up two cards, and if they are identical they are removed from the array. If not, they are both turned over again. To find matching pairs, players must remember the location of pictures previously exposed. Women managed to turn over all the cards in pairs with many fewer trials than men did.

Note that in the Eals and Silverman task, some objects exchanged locations, but no object was actually moved to a previously unoccupied position. Tom James in my lab asked whether there would still be a female advantage if some of the objects in the second array were moved

Figure 5.6
A variation on the response array of figure 5.5. The presentation array was identical to figure 5.5(a). Can you find the items that have changed location? In this response array items have been shifted into new locations. (From James and Kimura, 1997.)

into new locations previously unoccupied (figure 5.6). There was not. In his version of the test, men and women did not differ (James and Kimura, 1997). Women's scores were the same as in the original Eals task, but men's scores improved. James suggested that women's memory-for-location may be organized somewhat differently from men's. Women may be more likely to process object identity and object location together, that is, by overlapping brain systems; whereas men may tend to process the identity of an object and its location separately.

What might be the evolutionary basis of women's better memory for an object's location as shown in the Eals and Memory Game tasks? It is unlikely that knowing exactly where someone's good socks or the old green flashlight are has contributed significantly to the survival of women or their offspring. But it may be that the ability to detect small changes in the home environment did have a significant influence. If a predator or vermin has entered the home, noticing displacements of objects or changes in domestic space could help in detection of the intruder, and so contribute to survival.

It is also possible that, since ancestral females were less likely to travel long distances or be the navigators when they did travel, the necessity for locating objects outdoors would be limited to those within a short distance of the home base. This might promote the use of fixed landmarks, and/or the position of one object relative to other objects, as locator signs. In fact, for purposes of gathering food, it would be at least as useful to know that there is a plentiful berry supply near the jagged red rock or between it and the fallen maple tree, as to have a general cognitive map of the area. A cognitive map may allow a person to find the way from many different positions, but it may not be as precise.

The differences between men and women in finding their way through the environment, and the kinds of cues they appear to use, have an interesting parallel in rodents. In solving certain mazes, male rats tend to use *geometric* cues, such as the shape and dimensions of the room, whereas females rats rely more on landmark cues, such as the presence of objects near the maze (Williams, Barnett, and Meck, 1990). In rats these differences are determined by the early hormonal environment, to be discussed in more detail in chapter 9.

If men are better at one kind of spatial task, such as imaginal rotation, and women at another, such as memory for object location within an array, these must represent two relatively independent kinds of spatial ability. If they were simply different ways of sampling the *same* underlying ability, the sex differences would be in the same direction on the two tasks, that is, either men or women would be better on both. This shows how finding out about sex differences in cognitive abilities helps us discover other things about the way human abilities are organized.

In the appendix on dealing with number we mention another method for determining how abilities sort themselves out. For example, by using correlation techniques, we can learn which spatial tests are closely related to each other, and which are less closely related. Let's say that we gave two different "spatial" tests to a group of people and calculated the correlation between the scores on the two tests. The larger the correlation, the more closely related are the underlying abilities. If, on the other hand, we reliably get a correlation that is near zero, then we have to conclude that two different abilities are represented by the tests, even if in the past both have been labeled tests of "spatial" ability.

Yet another way to divide up spatial abilities is to see whether two groups of people who are known to be different in some objective way, such as sex, are equally "different" on various spatial tests. Usually this is done by means of *meta-analysis*, surveying a large number of published studies containing information on the sex and the performance of individuals on a wide variety of the tests of interest. If one kind of test consistently shows large sex differences (as measured by effect sizes) and another consistently shows small sex differences, then it may be that the two tests are measuring different abilities (Linn and Petersen, 1985). As we mentioned earlier, imaginal rotation tasks generally show large sex differences, whereas some other spatial tests do not. This finding has suggested that rotation is an ability separable from other spatial skills.

Using these and other methods, researchers have come up with the suggestion that there may be several distinct kinds of spatial abilities. Whether they are really clearly distinguishable abilities is still the topic of ongoing research. The labels used for these various abilities unfortunately vary from one writer to another. We employ the terminology on which there appears to be a consensus:

On the first two tasks listed below, the sex difference favoring males is large, sometimes approaching a full standard deviation (i.e., an effect size of 1.0).

1. *Targeting*, the ability to accurately hit a target, or to intercept a projectile (discussed in chapter 4).
2. *Spatial orientation*, which requires the subject to correct for changes in the orientation of an object, as in imaginal rotation, but does not involve imaginal manipulation of the parts within the figure. "Mental" rotation tasks like those in figure 5.1 are examples.
3. *Spatial location memory*, on which women excel under some circumstances (as in figure 5.5).

There is a modest-size sex difference on the next three types of tasks, favoring men:

4. *Spatial visualization*, which requires that we imagine what would happen when we fold, or put together, parts of an object. (Examples are the Paper Folding test, and the DAT Space Relations test, figure 5.7.)
5. *Disembedding*, sometimes included in spatial visualization, but arguably a different kind of function. This requires subjects to find a simple

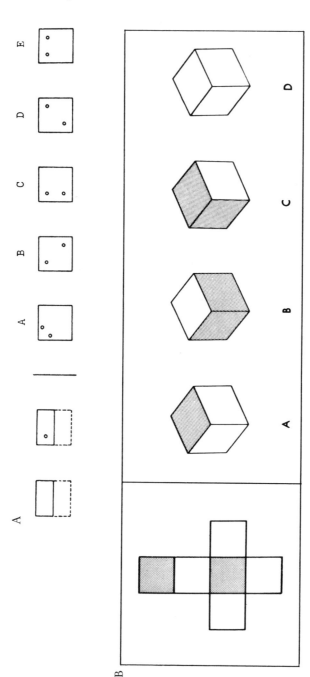

Figure 5.7
Spatial visualization tests: (a) An example from the Paper Folding test. The two figures on the left show how a square piece of paper has been folded, and a hole punched in it. When the paper is unfolded it looks like which figure on the right? (Answer: C) (Copyright 1962, 1975 by Educational Testing Service. All rights reserved. Reproduced under license. See Ekstrom, French, Harman, and Dermen, 1976.) (b) An example from DAT Space Relations test. The subject must decide which of the four figures depict the one on the left when it is folded up. (Answer: A) (From *Differential Aptitude Tests*, Form L, Space Relations subtest. Copyright 1947, 1948, 1972 by the Psychological Corporation. Reproduced by permission. All rights reserved.)

figure hidden in a more complex one (figure 5.8), and demands that they ignore much of the pattern in which the simple figure is "embedded." It thus may share some characteristics with the next ability, in that it requires shutting out extraneous information in order to accurately perform the task.

6. *Spatial perception (or, field independence)*, the ability to determine the real-world horizontal and vertical, often tested in the presence of distracting cues, such as a tilted frame. On one test of this ability, called the Rod-and-Frame test (figure 5.9), subjects view a rod within a frame that can be tilted at various angles, and are required either to set the rod to the true vertical, or to indicate when it has reached the vertical as the experimenter moves it gradually through small steps.

Another way to examine spatial perception is to present a series of tilted closed jars, one at a time (figure 5.10). The task for the subject is to draw a line depicting the water level in each one. Since water always settles in the horizontal, all that really needs to be done is to draw a horizontal line in each case. Yet, women consistently perform less well on this task than men do, and this effect has been seen in young and old subjects, and in both science and non-science university students (Robert and Harel, 1996).

There appear to be two main components to performance on the water-level task (Vasta, Lightfoot, and Cox, 1993). One is the ability to

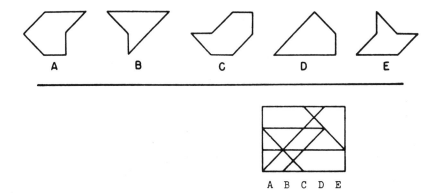

Figure 5.8
Disembedding: an example from the Hidden Figures test. The subject must find one of the five figures in the diagram below. (Hint: bottom right corner. Answer: D) (Copyright 1962, 1975 by Educational Testing Service. All rights reserved. Reproduced under license.)

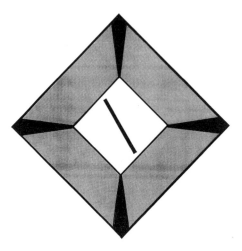

Figure 5.9
Depiction of the Rod-and-Frame test. The rod must be set to the vertical, ignoring the tilted frame.

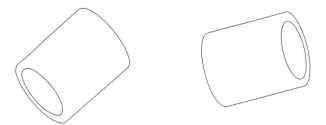

Figure 5.10
The Water Level task. The water line must be drawn in each jar.

maintain perception of the horizontal in the presence of a distracting framework (the tilt of the jar); the other is understanding the principle that water achieves a horizontal position at rest. Men and women who understand the principle do better at the task than those who do not, but even when the principle is explained to people, women still perform less well than men do. This seems to be due to their susceptibility to the tilted framework. If they are required to draw a horizontal line through an untilted rectangle or a circle (which of course has no tilt), their accuracy is much better, and does not differ from that of men.

In fact, Witkin (1967) suggested many years ago that both the Rod-and-Frame test and disembedding tasks sampled what he called "field independence." That is, people who are able to disregard the tilt of the frame, or to ignore the complex surround of the target figure, would be able to perform both tasks better than those who could not. On average, then, he assumed that women were more "field-dependent" than men, that is, more affected by the surrounding background.

The Role of Experience

Most of the comments in this section could apply equally well to other abilities described in the book. However, there has been more research on the role of experience in spatial abilities than on any other subset of abilities, with the exception of mathematics.

It seems reasonable to think that some of the difference among individuals in the various spatial talents, and in the math abilities described in the next chapter, is due to different life experiences. We have all seen the beneficial effects of practice in improving performance in particular activities, so we naturally tend to think that this advantage extends to all behaviors. Most of the significant "improvements" in performance we see with practice, however, could be regarded as either in the realm of motor skill (such as learning to ride a bicycle) or in devising strategies for solving a problem.

The improvement due to adoption of new strategies could be general or specific. An example of a general strategy in test taking is learning, after we have taken a few tests, that we should move on quickly to the next item if we cannot readily answer a question. So if people completely inexperienced with paper-and-pencil tests are compared on two occasions, their performance will almost always improve on the second occasion, regardless of the type of test.

Examples of more specific strategies would be realizing that variations on a word are acceptable in a "verbal fluency" task (e.g., "came" and "come"); or first rejecting obviously wrong matches in a spatial visualization task such as Paper Folding, and focusing on the remaining choices. None of these examples of the advantage of practice, however, need actually reflect improvement in the basic abilities—verbal fluency or vizualization. Much of the improvement could result from using these strategies.

Nevertheless, one may still ask whether there are significant changes in *ability level* determined by differing experiences. There are several ways to approach this question:

1. *Comparing children and adults.* If sex differences are only present in, or are substantially larger in, adults, this could (but doesn't necessarily) mean that they are a consequence of differential experiences between the sexes in the course of development.

It is often claimed that sex differences in cognitive abilities are either nonexistent or very small before puberty. Those who believe that most of the difference we see between men and women in problem-solving behavior is due to different life experiences point out that this position is consistent with the idea that the sexes diverge gradually as a result of socialization. However, even if it were true that sex differences did not appear until puberty, this would not in itself rule out a significant influence before puberty. As we saw in the chapter on sexual differentiation, some behaviors which do not appear until later in life have been determined or "organized" by the hormonal environment very early in life; albeit some of them may also need the priming provided by the hormonal surge just before puberty.

As it happens, however, there are some cognitive sex differences in children that parallel those in the adult. One reason they have not often been detected is that the kinds of tests (spatial tests, for example), used with children have not really measured the same abilities as those used with adults. In part this may have been due to the fact that children usually cannot do the *identical* tests that adults do. Another factor to contend with in children is that sex differences on such tests may be less robust because girls develop earlier than boys. So if we compare boys and girls of the same age, girls may have a slight overall advantage which may reduce the boys' edge on tasks on which they will later excel. For example, in a study in our lab, very young girls were better at a "disembedding" task (Lunn, 1987), though we know that in adults, men are more often superior.

Some evidence is emerging, however, which suggests that even before puberty, we may see sex differences favoring boys on a variety of spatial tasks (table 5.1). We mentioned in chapter 4 that at the very young ages of three-to-five years of age, we found boys to be more accurate at targeting than girls are. Another study of children in the same age range found that boys were faster at copying 3-dimensional models of outsize Lego pieces than girls were (McGuinness and Morley, 1991).

An extensive study looking at various aspects of the spatial abilities of children aged nine to thirteen used four different tests of spatial ability (Kerns and Berenbaum, 1991). One of the tests required children to imagine what a 3-dimensional object would look like if laid out flat (figure 5.11a). Another required them to use blocks to construct a structure pictured from an aerial and a frontal view (figure 5.11b). All of the tests showed a significant advantage for the boys.

In reviewing some of the literature, Johnson and Meade (1987) suggested that the early female precocity in language skills may mask the male superiority on a variety of spatial skills. They found that the latter appears around 10 years of age and persists throughout high school. Finally, a spatial rotation study of four- and five-year-olds, using a clock

Table 5.1
Prepubertal boys are better on some spatial and spatiomotor tasks

Rosser et al., 1984	Spatial rotation, ages 4–5
Johnson & Meade, 1987	Spatial tests, age 10+
Lunn, 1987	Throwing accuracy, ages 3–4
Kerns & Berenbaum, 1991	Spatial tests, ages 9–12
Vederhus & Krekling, 1996	Spatial tests, age 9

A

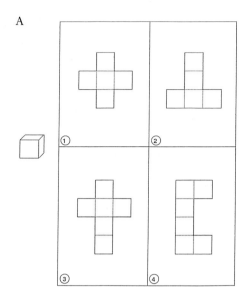

B

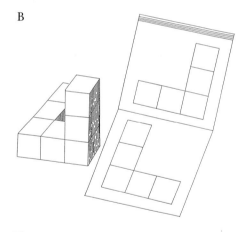

Figure 5.11
Two 3-dimensional tests used with children: (a) Geometric Forms: Which one of the four figures folds up to make a closed cube like the one shown on the left? (Answer: 3) (b) House Plans. Imagine building a house of blocks, which from the front looks like the top card; and from the top looks like the bottom card. The correct construction is shown on the left. (From Kerns and Berenbaum, 1991; (reprinted by permission of the authors from Tuddenham, 1970.)

face, found a similarly convincing advantage for boys (Rosser, Ensing, Glider, and Lane, 1984).

At these same early ages, girls are better at copying hand postures (chapter 4), better at verbal memory, and faster at color naming (chapter 8) than boys are.

2. *The effects of training or experience.* Another way to ask what role experience plays in producing these sex differences is to see whether intensive training changes the size of the difference. Admittedly, we would not expect a short period of training in an adult to be equivalent to a lifetime of experience; but we might still expect a small effect, with the performance of men and women moving closer together after such training. Performance on just about any task typically improves with practice, though as discussed above, whether the improvement is due to development of effective strategies or to actual increase in ability is uncertain.

Baenninger and Newcombe (1989) reviewed over twenty studies employing spatial tests in which both men and women were tested, and in which either some kind of practice or explicit training took place. They argued that if there is an upper limit to the benefits of experience, men would presumably be nearer that limit, and so should not benefit as much as women from additional training. They found, as expected, that in nearly all cases, scores improved as a result of training. However, both sexes improved equally. So it appears that short-term experience does not reduce the sex difference in spatial scores.

Other studies have asked whether current abilities are related to past life experience, that is, whether experience itself determined present abilities. Most such studies take the form of a questionnaire surveying subjects' past or present activities, and relating that information to scores on current tests. Some studies did in fact find a relation between the types of activities people recall engaging in—for example, various sports, repairing cars, using computer games—and certain spatial scores (Olson, Eliot, and Hardy, 1988). Unfortunately, the interpretation of such findings is entirely unclear. It is very probable that more spatially gifted individuals will, on average, take part in more spatially demanding activities than less gifted individuals. So any relationship seen may actually be demonstrating just the opposite of what is usually inferred from it. The abilities may in fact have determined the activities.

Some people have suggested that cognitive sex differences have been declining over the last several decades (Feingold, 1988). The authors of such studies argue that most of the difference between the sexes is due to socialization, and that since the difference in men's and women's environments has declined in recent years, the cognitive sex difference should also decline. We discuss some of the problems in trying to decide whether this is so in chapter 6 on mathematics. A difficult question still unanswered is whether the people (and tests) sampled over several decades are comparable; that is, whether over time, the composition of the groups of young men and women who take the aptitude tests has changed. For example, differing high school dropout rates for the sexes could mean that more below-average scorers of one sex are now taking the aptitude tests than in the past (Halpern, 1989).

However, in tests dealing specifically with imaginal rotation, there apparently has been no change in the sex difference over the past two decades (Masters and Sanders, 1993). We need more substantial information on this subject than we currently have.

3. *Comparing sex differences across cultures.* Different cultures put different constraints on the specific behaviors of males and females, and some of these constraints might be expected to affect cognitive function. Again we must caution that merely finding some cross-cultural variation does not in itself demonstrate that sex differences are culturally determined. Different cultural groups usually also have different gene pools, and may have evolved somewhat different sexual dimorphisms through their unique evolutionary history. Actual physical differences between the sexes also vary substantially from one race to another, indicating variation in hormonal dimorphism, and it is possible that cognitive differences parallel the physical dimorphisms.

The evidence is now quite clear that the male advantage on imaginal rotation tasks found in Western cultures is practically universal. It has been reported in African peoples (Mayes and Jahoda, 1988; Owen and Lynn, 1983), in East Indians (Owen and Lynn, 1983), and in Asians (Mann, Sasanuma, Sakuma, and Masaki, 1990). Information on other spatial tasks is meagre, but it appears that the male advantage on disembedding found in Western cultures is also present in some African groups (Berry, 1966).

Eskimos (the Inuit) are an apparent exception to the rule that men are better at spatial tasks than women. Two older studies reported finding no sex differences on various spatial tasks, including disembedding, in contrast to the differences found in Scottish and African samples (Berry, 1966; MacArthur, 1967). Although both authors interpreted the findings as evidence of cultural determination, an alternative explanation might invoke the evolutionary history of the Inuit. Their nomadic hunting life style in the bleak featureless landscape of the tundra regions might well have exerted strong selection pressures for women, as well as men, to develop significant spatial skills. Although Inuit women do not hunt, the demands of their day-to-day environment, which provides poor landmark information, might have favored evolution of alternative spatial abilities. Inuit women, unlike the women of most other North American aboriginal societies, are as likely as men to be artists and artisans. Unfortunately, we do not have factual information on Innuit targeting skills or imaginal rotation, the two skills showing the largest sex differences in Western cultures.

4. *Comparative studies.* Since male and female lab animals are usually housed and treated the same way, finding comparable sex differences in nonhuman and human species would make it more likely that human sex differences are also due to intrinsic factors. We mentioned in chapter 2 that male voles in some species perform better on certain mazes. The same is true of male rats and moreover, they tend to use geometric cues to find their way in a maze, whereas females tend to use landmark cues. In rats these differences are known to depend on differing early hormonal influences. Some researchers working with monkeys have shown parallel sex differences in human and monkey infants on two types of visual object identification tasks (Overman, Bachevalier, Schuhmann, and Ryan, 1996). A study of six baboons found that all three of the males could perform imaginal rotation tasks. However, two of the three female baboons were unable to do so (Vauclair, Fagot, and Hopkins, 1993).

Such studies indicate that male superiority on certain spatial tasks may be pervasive among mammals, because during their long evolutionary history, males generally travelled longer distances to find food or mates, or were responsible for guiding a family group. While modern men may experience no such necessity, our evolutionary heritage remains unchanged.

Summary

"Spatial" is a broad term, referring to a number of potentially separable abilities. Most spatial tests show some advantage for men, who excel particularly at imaginal rotation and targeting. Women, however, are generally better at recalling the positions of objects in an array, and at remembering landmarks along a route. It appears that men navigate primarily with reference to the geometric properties of space, whereas women tend more often to use specific objects to find their way.

Although it used to be thought that significant sex differences in spatial ability did not appear until puberty, there is now evidence that boys and girls differ at early ages, at least on tests of imaginal rotation and targeting. The evidence we have on the short-term effects of practice and training does not suggest that focused experience accounts for much of the difference. The reported relation between life activities and spatial ability is open to several interpretations. Moreover, recent cross-cultural studies indicate that sex differences on spatial tasks are also present in other cultures and races, though the magnitude of the difference may vary from culture to culture.

Finally, the presence of parallel sex differences in nonhuman species raises doubts about human child-rearing practices as a major influence on the sex difference in cognitive pattern.

Further Reading

Baenninger M. & Newcombe N. (1989) The role of experience in spatial test performance: a meta-analysis. *Sex Roles*, 20, 327–344.

Beatty W.W. & Troster A.I. (1987) Gender differences in geographical knowledge. *Sex Roles*, 16, 565–590.

Berry J.W. (1966) Temne and Eskimo perceptual skills. *International Journal of Psychology*, 1, 202–229.

Collins D.W. & Kimura D. (1997) A large sex difference on a two-dimensional mental rotation task. *Behavioral Neuroscience*, 111, 845–849.

Eals M. & Silverman I. (1994) The hunter-gatherer theory of spatial sex differences: proximate factors mediating the female advantage in recall of object arrays. *Ethology & Sociobiology*, 15, 95–105.

Ekstrom R.B., French J.W., Harman H.H. & Dermen D. (1976) *Kit of factor-referenced cognitive tests*. Princeton, N.J.: Educational Testing Service.

Feingold A. (1988) Cognitive gender differences are disappearing. *American Psychologist*, *43*, 95–103.

Galea L.A.M. & Kimura D. (1993) Sex differences in route learning. *Personality & Individual Differences*, *14*, 53–65.

Halpern D.F. (1989) The disappearance of cognitive gender differences: what you see depends on where you look. *American Psychologist*, *44*, 1156–1158.

James T.W. & Kimura D. (1997) Sex differences in remembering the locations of objects in an array: location-shifts versus location-exchanges. *Evolution & Human Behavior*, *18*, 155–163.

Johnson E.S. & Meade A.C. (1987) Developmental patterns of spatial ability: an early sex difference. *Child Development*, *58*, 725–740.

Kerns K.A. & Berenbaum S.A. (1991) Sex differences in spatial ability in children. *Behavior Genetics*, *21*, 383–396.

Linn M.C. & Petersen A.C. (1985) Emergence and characterization of sex differences in spatial ability: a meta-analysis. *Child Development*, *56*, 1479–1498.

Lunn D. (1987) *Foot asymmetry and cognitive ability in young children*. Unpublished Master's thesis, Department of Psychology, University of Western Ontario, London, Canada.

MacArthur R. (1967) Sex differences in field dependence for the Eskimo. *International Journal of Psychology*, *2*, 139–140.

Mann V.A., Sasanuma S., Sakuma N. & Masaki S. (1990) Sex differences in cognitive abilities: a cross-cultural perspective. *Neuropsychologia*, *28*, 1063–1077.

Masters M.S. & Sanders B. (1993) Is the gender difference in mental rotation disappearing? *Behavior Genetics*, *23*, 337–341.

Mayes J.T. & Jahoda G. (1988) Patterns of visual-spatial performance and 'spatial ability': dissociation of ethnic and sex differences. *British Journal of Psychology*, *79*, 105–119.

McBurney D.H., Gaulin S.J.C., Devineni T. & Adams C. (1997) Superior spatial memory of women: stronger evidence for the gathering hypothesis. *Evolution & Human Behavior*, *18*, 165–174.

McGuinness D. & Morley C. (1991) Sex differences in the development of visuo-spatial ability in pre-school children. *Journal of Mental Imagery*, *15*, 143–150.

Moffat S.D., Hampson E. & Hatzipantelis M. (1998) Navigation in a 'virtual' maze: sex differences and correlation with psychometric measures of ability in humans. *Evolution & Human Behavior*, *19*, 73–87.

Olson D.M., Eliot J. & Hardy R.C. (1988) Relationships between activities and sex-related differences in performance on spatial tests. *Perceptual & Motor Skills*, *67*, 223–232.

Overman W.H., Bachevalier J., Schuhmann E. & Ryan P. (1996) Cognitive gender differences in very young children parallel biologically based gender differences in monkeys. *Behavioral Neuroscience*, *110*, 673–684.

Owen K. & Lynn R. (1993) Sex differences in primary cognitive abilities among blacks, Indians and whites in South Africa. *Journal of Biosocial Science*, *25*, 557–560.

Robert M. & Harel F. (1996) The gender difference in orienting liquid surfaces and plumb lines: its robustness, its correlates, and the associated knowledge of simple physics. *Canadian Journal of Experimental Psychology*, *50*, 280–314.

Rosser R.A., Ensing S.S., Glider P.J. & Lane S. (1984) An information-processing analysis of children's accuracy in predicting the appearance of rotated stimuli. *Child Development*, *55*, 2204–2211.

Silverman I. & Eals M. (1992) Sex differences in spatial abilities: evolutionary theory and data. In J.H. Barkow, L. Cosmides & J. Tooby (Eds.), *The adapted mind*. New York: Oxford. pp. 533–549.

Tuddenham R.D. (1970) A Piagetian test of cognitive development. In W.B. Dockrell (Ed.), *On intelligence*. London: Methuen.

Vandenberg S.G. & Kuse A.R. (1978) Mental rotations, a group test of three-dimensional spatial visualization. *Perceptual & Motor Skills*, *47*, 599–601.

Vasta R., Lightfoot C. & Cox B.D. (1993) Understanding gender differences on the water-level problem: the role of spatial perception. *Merrill-Palmer Quarterly*, *39*, 391–414.

Vauclair J., Fagot J. & Hopkins W.D. (1993) Rotation of mental images in baboons when the visual input is directed to the left cerebral hemisphere. *Psychological Science*, *4*, 99–103. (Hopkins provided the information that 2 of the 3 female baboons could not do the task, and he reports that similar effects were found for the chimpanzee.)

Vederhus L. & Krekling S. (1996) Sex differences in visual spatial ability in 9-year-old children. *Intelligence*, *23*, 33–43.

Ward S.L., Newcombe N. & Overton W.F. (1986) Turn left at the church, or three miles north: a study of direction giving and sex differences. *Environment & Behavior*, *18*, 192–213.

Watson N.V. & Kimura D. (1991) Nontrivial sex differences in throwing and intercepting: relation to psychometrically-defined spatial functions. *Personality & Individual Differences*, *12*, 375–385.

Williams C.L., Barnett A.M. & Meck W.H. (1990) Organizational effects of early gonadal secretions on sexual differentiation in spatial memory. *Behavioral Neuroscience*, *104*, 84–97.

Witkin H.A. (1967) A cognitive-style approach to cross-cultural research. *International Journal of Psychology*, *2*, 233–250.

Wynn T.G., Tierson F.D. & Palmer C.T. (1996) Evolution of sex differences in spatial cognition. *Yearbook of Physical Anthropology*, *39*, 11–42.

6

Mathematical Aptitude

The difference between men and women in mathematical ability is one of the oldest-established findings in the area of sex differences. Yet it remains controversial. Since their inception, scores on a variety of high school and college entrance math aptitude tests have revealed a male advantage. On one of the most widely used aptitude tests, the Scholastic Aptitude Test–Mathematics component (SAT-M), the difference has remained fairly constant over the years at about one-half a standard deviation. This test, like other *aptitude* tests, is aimed at measuring abilities relatively independently of the courses that have been taken. It requires only the basic math skills most people taking the test would have been exposed to, but attempts to set problems they have not actually solved before.

However, if instead of aptitude tests, we look at students' grades in math courses throughout their school years, there is either no difference between males and females, or females get better marks (as indeed they tend to do in all subjects). Exactly why there is this discrepancy between math aptitude scores and school grades in math is not known, but we will discuss some possible explanations.

Some have argued that males' better performance on math aptitude tests is largely due to socialization factors, such as the different expectations teachers and parents supposedly have of the sexes, beginning early in life. This argument assumes that such attitudes determine the acquisition of math skills in children (rather than that the skills determine the attitudes). The fact that girls, if anything, get better marks in math courses than boys do, does not seem consistent with this explanation. Furthermore, the evidence for such differential expectations, on the part of teachers at least, is weak, a fact some critics explain by saying that teachers know they should not have such expectations and therefore do not report them.

Girls typically don't fare worse than boys on difficult *verbal* aptitude tests. So it is a question why different expectations for girls' and boys' math ability should arise, if not by experiencing different performance on the part of the two sexes. As we shall see shortly, the sex difference favoring males has been found in several cultures, and is not necessarily greater in more traditional societies (e.g., Japan), as one might expect from the socialization explanation.

An even more compelling argument against teachers' expectations as an explanation, however, is that girls are better at some aspects of math ability, and boys at others (something most teachers are unaware of). Throughout the school years girls tend to get better scores on the calculation or computation parts of aptitude tests, and boys on the parts requiring mathematical problem solving (Hyde, Fennema, and Lamon, 1990; Jensen, 1988). Since *these skills are taught together in the same class by the same teacher*, it is difficult to see how a teacher's general expectations, or how treatment of boys and girls in math classes, could be a significant factor in producing such opposite results.

One of the arguments given in favor of socialization factors is that sex differences in math aptitude (as in other areas) may be decreasing over decades (Feingold, 1988; Hyde et al., 1990). The suggestion is that as boys and girls are treated more alike, a reasonable expectation would be that their skills will become more alike. An analysis of math scores over a large number of studies and a 20-year span (Hyde et al., 1990) did indeed suggest that sex differences were decreasing. Unfortunately, it is difficult to interpret "meta-analyses" of this kind unless one knows how comparable the tests are over any function, such as time. For example, if older samples contained more tests of "mathematical reasoning" than the more recent ones, an apparent change might appear over time which is actually an artifact of the particular kinds of tests being sampled. Most of the studies sampled by Hyde do not provide enough information about the test characteristics to enable us to decide. An analysis of standardized tests done on a few large samples is more convincing (Feingold, 1988). It showed a decline in the size of the sex difference over decades on a junior version of the SAT-Math (PSAT), but not on the adult version. Others (Benbow, 1988; Reisberg, 1998) also find no decline in the sex difference on the SAT.

To demonstrate a real decrease in the sex difference over decades requires that we compare the sexs on the same, or nearly the same *items* of a test, and also groups of the same *ethnic and sex composition*. However, items on tests like the SAT (and many other standardized tests) change over the years, because some items go out of fashion, or even because items performed better by one sex were deleted! We need to know that changes like these are not the basis of declines in group differences. Similarly, a large change in the ethnic composition of the test-takers might change the apparent size of the sex difference. For example, if later decades had a higher proportion of Asian or black test-takers, the sex difference might be smaller, because these groups generally show smaller sex differences than whites do. Halpern (1989) has pointed out that the dropout rate for high school students has been shifting over time, from a greater proportion of girls in earlier years to a higher proportion of boys more recently. If less gifted individuals of one sex are dropping out of (or staying in) high school, this could change the magnitude of sex differences on a variety of tests. So the question of changes over time is a very complex one, and is not by any means resolved.

Comparing sex differences in math skills across cultures is another way of understanding how they are determined, although it is complicated by the diversity of teaching methods, curricula, and so forth. Nevertheless international comparisons have attempted to measure the overall math skills of students in different countries. The standardized tests employed in these comparisons are also appropriate for making comparisons between the sexes. Because of the different findings for computation and problem-solving skills, cross-cultural studies that do not break down overall scores into these components are less useful for understanding what is going on.

Within the United States, sex differences in math vary somewhat according to racial origin. The sex differences appear to be larger in Caucasians than in blacks and Asians, but are present in all three groups (Benbow, 1988; Jensen, 1988). There is no simple relationship between overall performance and size of sex difference, since Asians have higher, and blacks lower scores than whites. Some have argued that the fact that the size of the sex difference varies across racial or ethnic group casts doubt on a biological contribution to the differences. But it is clear that there are also physiological/biological differences across races that might interact with sex in such a way as to result in variation in the degree of difference. We will return to this later when we talk about possible biological mechanisms.

A study comparing very large numbers of 13-year-old boys and girls in the United States and Thailand (Engelhard, 1990) reports that girls in both countries are better at the computational components of math tests, whereas boys are better at the problem-solving components. Similar patterns are found in a comparison of elementary school children in the United States, Taiwan and Japan (Lummis and Stevenson, 1990). So it appears, although our information is somewhat limited, that there is some consistency across cultures and races (see table 6.1).

It may seem strange, from an evolutionary perspective, that there are consistent sex differences in math reasoning, since formal mathematics has a very short human history. However, we can probably assume that many of the relational problems which are posed in math reasoning tasks were encountered in everyday life for millions of years. For example, the ability to see that a 5-foot plus 7-foot tree trunk would be longer than an 8-foot plus 3-foot trunk must have been with us for a very long time, even though not laid out in formal symbols.

What do we mean by math problem solving? Knowing that males score higher on math reasoning tests is not in itself very informative. What precisely differentiates the sexes in this regard is still a question under investigation. Although some have suggested that the male advantage in math derives from superior spatial, especially 3-dimensional rotational ability (e.g., Geary, 1996), there is little factual support for the idea that this is the critical component. In our own studies of university undergraduates, math reasoning is no more highly related to scores on a spatial rotation test than it is to vocabulary scores. This suggests that 3-D rotational ability may not contribute any more to math skill than does general intelligence.

In fact, a common theme running through studies on this question is that those who perform very well on so-called math reasoning tests are

Table 6.1
Some sex differences in math components across cultures and ethnic groups

Author	Subject Groups	Findings
Campbell, 1991	USA: Asian, Caucasian	Males better than females on SAT-Math, in both groups.
Engelhard, 1990	USA, Thailand	Boys better on application of problem, girls on computation.
Lummis et al., 1990	USA, China, Japan	Boys better at math word problems.
Jensen, 1988	USA: blacks, Asians, whites	Girls better at computation, boys at concepts and applications.
Chipman, 1988	USA: 13-year-olds	Girls better on computation, boys on problem-solving.
Moore et al., 1987	USA- blacks, whites, Hispanics	On Math Knowledge, females better in early years, males later on. Whites show largest sex difference.
Marshall et al., 1987	USA; grades 3 and 6	Girls better at computation, boys at problem application.

also better able to translate the verbally stated problems into a framework that can be solved numerically. In one study (Dark and Benbow, 1990), subjects were to rewrite the statement "Randy has three times as many transformers as gobots" in a form in which "T" represents transformers, and "G" gobots. Actual solution of the problem was not required. Another example of these transformation problems is "In the dormitory cafeteria, for every four people who take cake, five people take ice cream." Another kind of rewriting problem presented is the "story", e.g., "The entertainment portion of a 30-minute program lasted 4 minutes longer than 4 times the portion devoted to advertising." Individuals gifted in math appeared, perhaps surprisingly, better able to make such translations than verbally gifted individuals, particularly when they had to translate complex relational statements.

A series of studies (e.g., Low and Over 1993) found that *even when high school males and females were matched on overall math ability*, males were better than females at devising correct solutions to algebraic word problems. Males were better at recognizing occasions when the data given were insufficient to solve the problem, and at ignoring facts irrelevant to the solution. An example of a problem with missing information is "Alba invested a certain amount of money at 6% annual interest and another amount at 8% interest. Last year she received $580 in interest. How much did she invest at each rate?" When there were no missing or irrelevant facts, differences between the matched groups were minimal or absent.

These sex differences on word problems are the more puzzling, since on strictly verbal reasoning tasks, males and females do not usually differ significantly. The finding that girls are better able to perform computations and boys better able to solve word problems has been interpreted by some as indicating that females tend to approach math problems in a more "automatized" fashion (Marshall and Smith, 1987). That is, they tend to rely more on previously used solutions.

Another approach to studying the nature of the sex differences in mathematics has been to consider *cognitive complexity* (Engelhard, 1990). According to this schema, computation is considered least complex, comprehension or understanding the question is next in complexity, and application (finding the correct solution), is the most complex task. In the large-scale study comparing 13-year-olds in United States and Thailand, girls did better on items emphasizing computation, while boys excelled in application. There were no significant differences in comprehension. The patterns were very similar in the two countries, suggesting that they were not primarily influenced by cultural factors.

One proposed source of differences between the sexes on math problems is that the content of math problems is biased in favor of males. If items employ predominantly male protagonists, or activities usually associated with males rather than females, females might find them less familiar, and possibly less appealing. No convincing case has been made for this assertion, however; in fact studies that have systematically used word problems favoring females ("Martha is making square cookies") or males ("Mark is cutting square pieces of sod") find that the gender bias has no influence on scores. Males perform better on female-biased, male-biased, and neutral items (Chipman, Marshall, and Scott, 1991; Sappington, Larsen, Martin, and Murphy, 1991).

Another interpretation is that females suffer more from "math anxiety" than males do, so they perform less well on math aptitude tests. One might question why such anxiety would not extend to school math exams, where girls do at least as well as boys. The occasional attempt to relate someone's degree of "math anxiety" to career choices or SAT scores has been inconclusive or has failed to control for subjects' general level of test-taking anxiety, that is, in other subjects (Chipman, Krantz and Silver, 1992). One study that looked at girls' and boys' anxiety about their courses found no support for a math-specific effect (Felson and Trudeau, 1991). Girls were more anxious about all courses than boys were, yet got better grades in their math courses (but as usual, lower scores on a math aptitude test).

It is often claimed that group differences in math (both ethnic and sex differences) result from differences in number and kind of courses taken (e.g., Moore and Smith, 1987). The sex difference in math aptitude increases with increasing age and grade levels, becoming most marked and consistent at the senior high school and college levels. Because the number of math courses taken by young men and women also diverges at these ages, this has seemed to be a logical explanation. But recall our cautions about correlational data. Even if we find a significant correlation between math courses taken and scores on math aptitude tests, does this in itself tell us that the courses taken are having an effect on the scores? Not at all. It is quite possible that it is the other way around; that is, students who do well in math are on average more likely to enjoy math and are therefore more likely to take additional courses.

The same cautions should be applied to claims such as: (1) parental expectations influence math performance (perhaps the child's performance influences parental expectation), (2) teachers' expectations influence success in math and/or lab courses (perhaps the students' performance influences the teacher's expectations), (3) students' self-confidence in their math ability affects their success in math (perhaps confidence comes from previously high achievement and so merely reflects ability levels). And so on.

The interest in mathematical ability has been greatly heightened in recent years by indications that math aptitude predicts success in many fields of science and technology. For example, the young people identified by Benbow's Study of Mathematically Precocious Youth are much more likely than the general college population to choose science as a career. Underrepresentation of women, blacks and Hispanics in science fields in the United States has been related to their lower scores on math tests. It has even been suggested (Hacker, 1983) that males have imposed mathematics as a requirement for admission to engineering as a means of keeping women out!

An intriguing study published in the Harvard Educational Review (Wainer and Steinberg, 1992) shows that SAT-M scores actually predict grades on college math tests extremely well, for both men and women (see table 6.2). The SAT-M scores of those who subsequently get Cs, Bs, As, etc., in math courses show a predictable progression upward. The same is true for course complexity. Students who took more difficult math courses had higher Sat-M scores, on average, than those who took less advanced courses. These tidy relationships hold for both men and women, as we said. But the puzzle is that the women who on average had, as usual, lower SAT-M scores than men, did not have lower grades.

So the SAT predicts college math course grades within the sexes, but does not predict very well between the sexes. The pattern reported throughout the school years is now showing up in advanced math courses. Why is it that women are doing significantly less well on the aptitude tests, yet are getting just as good grades in advanced math? Is it that women, on average, are more organized in their study habits, and/or that they write better exams? Do they work harder, or are they more motivated to get good grades? Or is it that they do better when dealing with material that is familiar, where solutions have already been presented and novel problem solving is not required? We don't yet know the answers to these questions.

Regardless of the answers, such findings have raised the issue of whether women and men should meet exactly equivalent SAT-M stand-

Table 6.2
Relation between grades in math courses and scores on SAT-Math in male and female first-year college students.

Men: Mean SAT-Math scores

Grade	Advanced Math	Calculus	Regular Math
A	713	635	586
B	686	615	543
C	666	597	518
D	642	580	503
F	651	579	492

Women: Mean SAT-Math scores

Grade	Advanced Math	Calculus	Regular Math
A	677	604	540
B	665	580	501
C	631	559	475
D	611	540	448
F	600	537	448

After Wainer & Steinberg, 1992.

ards for admission to a variety of college programs. This question is a difficult one to answer, but one must keep in mind that grades are not the ultimate goal of an education, and therefore not the ultimate measure of the validity of an aptitude test. The long-term measure of validity, the thing we are usually trying to predict with such aptitude tests, is a person's competence in an occupation or profession and the consequent impact he or she has on the world. If SAT-M scores *do* predict career success for certain jobs, especially across the sexes, it would be reasonable to maintain identical admission standards.

For example, several studies have shown that female scientists are on the whole less productive than comparable male scientists (Cole, 1987; Long, 1993). They "tend not to publish as much as males who are of equal professional age, who come from similar educational backgrounds, and who are in the same specialties" (Cole, 1987). Productivity and impact in one's field, which can be gauged by how often one's research is referred to by other scientists (Rushton, 1989), are critical measures of success in science. The facts suggest that on average, women who do enter the field of science are less successful than men.

Considerable concern has been expressed about the "gender imbalance" in the sciences. Many people have concluded that certain fields of science (and technological fields such as engineering) discriminate against women, and that this is why there are fewer women in these fields. They argue that the sciences, particularly the physical sciences, are a white male bastion dedicated to keeping women out. According to one writer, "Physics, even more than other sciences, seems unfriendly to females" (Brush, 1991). Why anyone should imagine that such a conspiracy could be maintained in a manifestly egalitarian discipline is never made clear. Science, more than most disciplines, has quite explicit rules of evidence and fairly objective criteria for excellence. We might therefore expect success in science to be, if anything, *more* rather than less related to merit, than in other areas of scholarship.

Looking at specific fields of science gives us some clues about what may be happening. A U.S. National Science Foundation survey ("Biennial PhD survey," 1991) of all persons with doctoral degrees working in the sciences found that the percentage of women working in the physical sciences and engineering was much lower than in biological (including medical) and social sciences. As shown in table 6.3, in both physics and engineering, fewer than 5 percent of doctoral workers were women, compared to almost 25 percent in biology. This pattern is found in other countries as well, although the precise numbers vary from country to country (Benditt, 1994).

Does this really mean that physical scientists are especially discriminatory? Or is there some other explanation? We can get a partial answer to this question by looking at the representation of Asians in these same fields. At the time of the survey, Asians constituted less than 3 percent of the U.S. population, but were overrepresented in all fields of science except psychology. In fact, in engineering their ratio was almost 20 percent! At the same time, blacks, who constituted approximately 15 percent of the population, filled fewer than 5 percent of the positions in every field of science. Since Asians are doing so well, it is difficult to

Table 6.3
Representation of women and Asian minorities in biology compared with math-oriented sciences

Field	% Women	% White	% Asian
Biology	23.4	90.7	5.3
Math/Science	8.7	88.7	9.3
Physics/Astronomy	4.7	89.8	8.5
Engineering	3.1	79.1	19.5

After Science, 1991

reconcile these numbers with explanations based on discrimination against nonwhite, nonmale groups.

A more probable explanation is that mathematical reasoning ability is an especially significant determinant of success in the physical sciences. Benbow (1988) has reported that the ratio of males to females at the high end of the SAT-M scale is over ten to one. This fits rather well with the proportion of men to women in fields emphasizing math. Similarly, it is known that Asians score higher, on average, than whites, and whites than blacks (e.g., Lerner and Nagai, 1996; Reisberg, 1998). This finding could effectively account for the high proportion of Asians in math-oriented fields. So while there may indeed be "discrimination" in the fields of physical sciences it may simply be discrimination on the basis of a specific ability.

Of course, ability is unlikely to be the sole determinant of anyone's choice of profession. Even women with very superior math scores tend to choose physical science careers less often than men do. One important reason for this appears to be that most women, including many with excellent math skills, have more person-oriented than object-oriented values, in contrast to equivalently gifted men (Lubinski and Benbow, 1992). So that even though such women might be able to succeed in science fields, their interests may dictate otherwise.

Summary

On average, males get higher scores on mathematical reasoning or problem-solving *aptitude* tests, whereas females do better on tests involving computation. In contrast, on school achievement tests (including math achievement), girls generally do better than boys. The sex differences are apparent in elementary school but appear to become more marked in higher grades. Since both aspects of math are taught by the same person, teacher-related factors are unlikely to be the explanation for these differences. Nor do other "socialization" explanations such as gender bias in problem content, math anxiety, parental expectation, and so on, adequately account for the differences.

In comparable tests across countries and ethnic groups, the sex differences appear in all groups, though they tend to be smaller in Asians and blacks. Suggestions that sex differences are declining over decades are difficult to evaluate in the light of changes in test items, and in ethnic and sex composition of test-takers. The demonstrated relation between math aptitude and number of math courses taken is open to various interpretations.

Math aptitude has been linked to success in science and technology, especially in those sciences that employ math to a greater degree. The "underrepresentation" of women in such fields has sometimes been attributed to discrimination from a white male majority, but the disproportionately high representation of Asians in these fields makes this an unlikely explanation. Choice of occupation appears to differ markedly between the sexes, even among the math-gifted, with highly able women nevertheless preferring more person-oriented occupations.

Further Reading

Benbow C.P. (1988) Sex differences in mathematical reasoning ability in intellectually talented preadolescents: Their nature, effects, and possible causes. *Behavioral & Brain Sciences, 11*, 169–232.

Benditt J., Ed., (1994) Women in science '94. Comparisons across cultures. *Science, 263*, 1391–1496.

Biennial PhD survey of the National Science Foundation. (1991) *Science, 252*, 1112–1117.

Brush S.G. (1991) Women in science and engineering. *American Scientist, 79*, 404–419. (Quotation is from page 404.)

Campbell J.R. (1991) The roots of gender inequity in technical areas. *Journal of Research in Science Teaching, 28*, 251–264.

Chipman S.F., Marshall S.P. & Scott P.A. (1991) Content effects on word problem performance: A possible source of test bias? *American Educational Research Journal, 28,* 897–915.

Chipman S.F., Krantz D.H. & Silver R. (1992) Mathematics anxiety and science careers among able college women. *Psychological Science, 3,* 292–295.

Cole J.R. (1987) Women in science. In D.N. Jackson & J.P. Rushton (Eds.), *Scientific excellence.* Newbury Park: Sage Publications, pp. 359–375. (Quotation is from page 366.)

Dark V.J. & Benbow C.P. (1990) Enhanced problem translation and short-term memory: components of mathematical talent. *Journal of Educational Psychology, 82,* 420–429.

Engelhard G. (1990) Gender differences in performance on mathematics items: evidence from USA and Thailand. *Contemporary Educational Psychology, 15,* 13–16.

Feingold A. (1988) Cognitive gender differences are disappearing. *American Psychologist, 43,* 95–103.

Felson R.B. & Trudeau L. (1991) Gender differences in mathematics performance. *Social Psychology Quarterly, 54,* 113–126.

Geary D.C. (1996) Sexual selection and sex differences in mathematical abilities. *Behavioral & Brain Sciences, 19,* 229–247.

Hacker S.L. (1983) Mathematization of engineering: limits on women and the field. In J. Rothschild (Ed.), *Machina ex dea. Feminist perspectives on technology.* New York: Pergamon. pp. 38–58.

Halpern D.F. (1989) The disappearance of cognitive gender differences: What you see depends on where you look. *American Psychologist, 44,* 1156–1158.

Hyde J.S., Fennema E. & Lamon S.J. (1990) Gender differences in mathematics performance: a meta-analysis. *Psychological Bulletin, 107,* 139–155.

Jensen A.R. (1988) Sex differences in arithmetic computation and reasoning in prepubertal boys and girls. *Behavioral & Brain Sciences, 11,* 198–199.

Lerner R. & Nagai A.K. (1996) Racial preferences at U.C. Berkeley. *Center for Equal Opportunity,* 15 October.

Long J.S. (1993) Measures of sex differences in scientific productivity. *Social Forces, 71,* 159–178.

Low R. & Over R. (1993) Gender differences in solution of algebraic word problems containing irrelevant information. *Journal of Educational Psychology, 85,* 331–339.

Lubinski D. & Benbow C.P. (1992) Gender differences in abilities and preferences among the gifted: implications for the math-science pipeline. *Current Directions in Psychological Science, 1,* 61–66.

Lummis M. & Stevenson H.W. (1990) Gender differences in beliefs and achievement: a cross-cultural study. *Developmental Psychology, 26,* 254–263.

Marshall S.P. & Smith J.D. (1987) Sex differences in learning mathematics: a longitudinal study with item and error analyses. *Journal of Educational Psychology*, 79, 372–383.

Moore E.G.J. & Smith A.W. (1987) Sex and ethnic group differences in mathematical achievement: results from the national longitudinal study. *Journal for Research in Mathematics Education*, 18, 25–36.

Reisberg L. (1998) Disparities grow in SAT scores of ethnic and racial groups. *The Chronicle of Higher Education*, 11 September, A42.

Rushton J.P. (1989) A ten-year scientometric revisit of British psychology departments. *The Psychologist: Bulletin of the British Psychological Society*, 2, 64–68.

Sappington J., Larsen C., Martin J. & Murphy K. (1991) Sex differences in math problem solving as a function of gender-specific content. *Educational & Psychological Measurement*, 51, 1041–1048.

Wainer H. & Steinberg L.S. (1992) Sex differences in performance on the Mathematics section of the Scholastic Aptitude Test: a bidirectional validity study. *Harvard Educational Review*, 62, 323–335.

7

Perception

The kind of information we take in from the external world depends in part on our senses (vision, hearing, touch, taste, smell, etc.), and in part on the way the brain deals with the input from our sense organs. Do men and women differ in their basic sensory experience, that is, in the raw material from which we build our representations of the world? The answer seems to be that women are generally more sensitive, in that they can detect lower levels of stimulation in all senses except vision.

Taste is usually divided into four main categories, based on different receptors on the tongue—sweet, sour, salt, and bitter. Adult women show greater sensitivity to all four tastes than do adult men (Velle, 1987), and they appear more consistently to identify tastes. Women also show greater sensitivity to most smells, especially those having a musklike odor. Sensitivity to taste and smell varies with changing hormone levels during the menstrual cycle and pregnancy. This variation, and the fact that the sex differences in sensitivity may not appear before puberty, suggest that some of the sex difference is related to the distinctive hormonal makeup of men and women.

Auditory sensitivity is typically measured by determining at how low a volume a person can hear a "pure" tone, that is, one limited to a single frequency. This *pure tone threshold* is lower in women than in men, meaning that their hearing is more sensitive throughout the range of sounds humans can hear, but it is especially marked at frequencies above four thousand cycles per second. This difference could be due entirely to a more sensitive inner ear. Again, the differences appear greater in adults than in children. However, this greater sensitivity doesn't seem to give any advantage to women in distinguishing between two tones of differing frequencies (*pitch discrimination*). On pitch discrimination, which depends on activity in the auditory centers of the brain, men and women do not appear to be very different. Women, however, find noise unpleasantly loud at lower levels of stimulation than men do (McGuinness, 1972).

Although there is less information about the sense of touch, women may be more sensitive in this modality as well. The simplest way to measure this is by pressing filaments of differing thickness on the skin, and recording whether the person feels anything or not. With very fine hairlike filaments, most people don't report any sensation, but as the filaments used get thicker, more people report feeling something, and everyone, except people with damage to their nervous systems, feels the thickest stimuli. There is some evidence that females are slightly more sensitive than males, and one study found such a trend also in children (Ghent-Braine, 1961; Weinstein and Sersen, 1961). Because these differences are at least as large on the arms as the hands, they can't be explained by the fact that men may have more callouses on their hands.

So there is evidence that women show greater sensitivity to stimuli of various kinds. But what do we find if we look at how this information is put together to form a familiar percept, such as a specified fragrance, an identifiable sound or the taste of a familiar food? We have already suggested that women's more sensitive hearing apparently doesn't help them in telling apart two different pure tones, so we wouldn't necessarily expect to find sex differences in the ability to put sensory information together. Other than some evidence that women may be better able than men to identify forms by touch than are men, we actually know very little about sex differences in modalities except vision.

Vision

Sex differences in vision are somewhat mixed. One way to rate vision is to measure the extent of a person's visual field, that is, how far out to the periphery one can see while fixating the gaze on a central point. Women have slightly larger visual fields than men do (Burg, 1968). Another way to evaluate vision is to rate how small an object a person can see within the visual field, an ability called *acuity*. Men are better on acuity measures than women are (Burg, 1966). Yet another basic visual ability is sensitivity to flicker. If a light is turned on and off repeatedly, we can detect the on-off phases until the alternation between them becomes too rapid. This point is called the *critical flicker fusion threshold*. Men can detect the flicker at faster alternation rates than women can (Ginsburg, Jurenovskis, and Jamieson, 1982).

We know that women name colors more quickly than men do, and there is a general belief that women are more attuned to color. (The female advantage in color naming is discussed further in the next chapter.) Strangely enough, however, there seems to be no information on sex differences in sensitivity to color nor even on the ability to tell the difference between two closely related colors. Men are more likely to suffer from color blindness, but subtler differences between the sexes have not been examined.

In chapter 5 on spatial abilities, we talked about men's superiority in appreciation of the true vertical and horizontal. This was measured by the Rod-and-Frame test, in which a line had to be positioned in the vertical (or horizontal) within a tilted frame, and by the Water-Level task, where subjects must draw the water line in jars tilted at various angles (see figure 5.10). Both tests require that the subject ignore a surrounding framework in making decisions. Women appear to be especially sensitive to such frameworks, a state called "field dependence" by some researchers (Witkin, 1967), meaning that they seem less able than men to make their judgments independent of the surrounding irrelevant input.

Generalizing from these studies, Dewar (1967) predicted that women might show greater susceptibility to a perceptual illusion, called the *Müller-Lyer illusion* (figure 7.1). Most people see the line with the arrow arms going outward as longer than the line with the arms pointing inward, although the lines are actually the same length. The study participants were asked to repeatedly set the length of a series of such lines so that they appeared equal, by means of an apparatus on which they could adjust the length of one of the figures. Typically, as the subject performs this task over several trials, the illusion weakens. Arguing that this illusion might be similar to the influence of the tilted frame in the Rod-and-Frame test, Dewar predicted and found that in women the illusion did not decline over repeated trials as rapidly as it did in men.

Rhonda Peterson (1993) from my lab, in searching for some basic visual correlates of the male superiority on spatial rotation tasks, investigated sex differences in stereoscopic vision. One of the most important pieces of

Figure 7.1
The Müller-Lyer illusion. To most people, the line with the open arrows (top) appears longer than the bottom line, even though they are the same length.

information we have about the distance of an object from us comes from the different pictures we get of it from our two eyes (figure 7.2). Since the eyes are several centimeters apart, the image of any object is slightly different for the left and right retina. The closer an object is to us, the greater the difference between the images to the two eyes. You can test this yourself by holding an object at different distances and closing each eye in turn. The object "jumps" more, indicating a bigger difference between the picture received by the two eyes, when it is held near you than when it is held farther away. The brain uses this difference between eyes, the *binocular disparity*, to provide information about the object's position in space. Fusing the images from the two eyes gives us the perception of depth.

We asked, since men have reputedly better 3-dimensional *spatial* ability than women do, whether this superiority might be related to a basic visual function such as the stereoscopic fusion of the two retinal images. There are several ways to test this hypothesis, all of them requiring slightly different and separate input to left and right eyes. One method is to ask the viewer whether two figures that look flat when visible to either eye alone are seen "in depth" when presented by means of a stereoscope. The stereoscope separates the input to the two eyes and allows us to present two slightly different views of a picture to the two eyes, simulating what happens naturally with binocular vision. The experience of depth results from fusion of the two inputs in the brain.

Another method is to separate the inputs to the two eyes by using a red filter over one eye and a green filter over the other, while the subject views a matrix of mixed red and green points. The red and green components of the picture are shifted in such a way that they correspond, respectively, to the degree of disparity between the images we would experience in

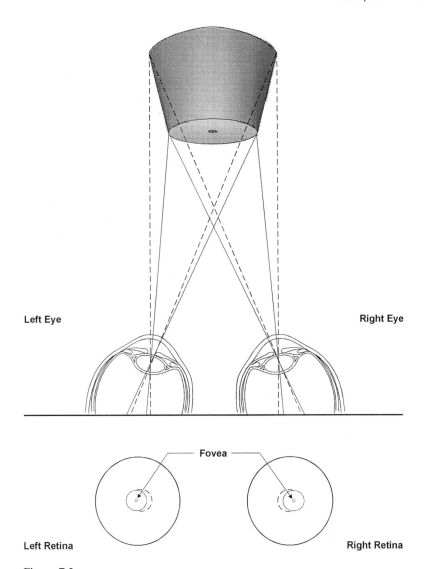

Figure 7.2
Example of binocular disparity, showing how the picture of the object is not the same in the two eyes.

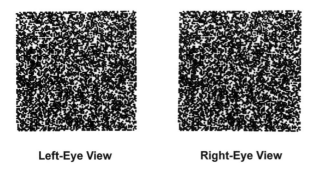

Left-Eye View   **Right-Eye View**

Figure 7.3
Example of a random-dot stereogram. Part of the display is appropriately shifted relative to the other eye, to simulate natural binocular disparity. The viewer looking through a stereoscope, which keeps the two eye-inputs separate, sees a figure floating in front of the background, in this case, a triangle. (After Julesz, 1964.)

normal viewing with both eyes open. The 3-D glasses sometimes used as toys employ similar methods.

Yet another way to use the stereoscope is to present apparently random dot patterns to each eye, but with a subarea of one eye slightly shifted relative to the other eye, again simulating normal disparity (Julesz, 1964) (figure 7.3). The advantage of this method is that we don't have to rely on the viewer's subjective report of "depth." If the images from the two eyes do not fuse, nothing will be seen, but if they do fuse, a figure will appear to "float" in front of the square.

To our surprise, we found that, although the differences between men and women were not large, women consistently either gave more accurate report of the images presented to the eyes, or identified the fused images more quickly. Although the men in the same sample showed the usual superiority on 3-D spatial rotation tasks, there was no consistent relationship between performance on the stereoscopic and spatial rotation tests. Since then we have learned of another similar study (Joseph, 1996) in which women identified numbers presented via random-dot stereograms more quickly than men did.

One report finds that infant girls show an early preference for patterns to the two eyes that either can be fused, or that result in reports of depth in adults (Gwiazda, Bauer, and Held, 1989). Baby girls show such preferences at nine to ten weeks of age, while boys do so only at twelve to thirteen weeks. As we have already mentioned, some sex differences favoring girls disappear later in life, but this may be one that lasts.

Why should women show better stereoscopic vision than men? This seems paradoxical, in view of men's generally better visual acuity and the presumed role of sexual division of labour in the evolution of men's superior spatial ability. Our studies on stereopsis simulated distances fairly close to the body, and it is possible that with longer distances, the female advantage would disappear. It has been suggested that stereopsis is particularly important for directing fine movements within personal space. Since women tend to excel at such movements (as discussed in chapter 4), it may well be that their better use of binocular disparity evolved along with their fine motor control. However, with increasing distance of an object from the body, the images to the two eyes are less different, so that binocular disparity is less useful as a cue.

Finally, there is another kind of visual perceptual skill, referred to as "perceptual speed" on which women are usually superior. This term refers to the ability to make rapid comparisons among a number of designs (letters, numbers, or pictures). On one test of this kind, Identical Pictures (figure 7.4), the task is simply to find the figure that is identical

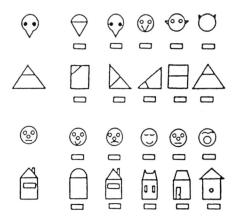

Figure 7.4
Identical Pictures test. The subject must decide which picture is identical to the one on the left. There are many items, and the subject is instructed to proceed as quickly as possible. (From Ekstrom et al., 1976. Copyright 1962, 1975 by Educational Testing Service. All rights reserved. Reproduced under license.)

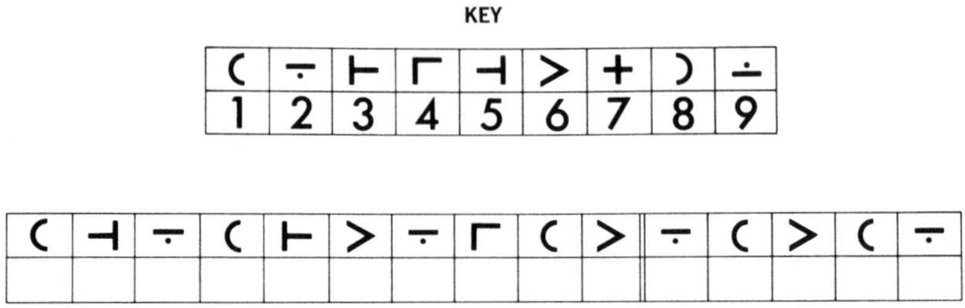

KEY

Figure 7.5
Symbol-Digit test. The subject must, as quickly as possible, fill in the appropriate digit in the spaces below. On the actual test, a full page of such items must be completed. (From Smith, 1967. Material from the *Symbol Digit Modalities Test* copyright 1973 by Western Psychological Services. Reprinted by permission of the publisher, Western Psychological Services, 12031 Wilshire Boulevard, Los Angeles, California 90025, U.S.A. Not to be reprinted in whole or in part for any additional purpose without the expressed, written permission of the publisher. All rights reserved.)

to a target item. On others, such as the Digit Symbol subtest of the Wechsler Adult Intelligence Scale (Wechsler, 1958), or the similar Symbol-Digit test (Smith, 1967) (figure 7.5), a single number and a symbol are paired in an array visible throughout the test, and the task is to fill in the appropriate number or symbol in each blank space below.

Obviously, there are several behavioral components to such tasks, including scanning, writing or marking an answer, and even immediate memory. One author (Majeres, 1983) suggested that the critical factor in the female advantage on such tasks is the ability to verbalize the stimuli; that is, to assign a name to each. However, women in his study were also better than men when matching a series of the letter F in differing orientations, in which labeling the forms (all called "F") would not help. So although being able to verbalize the items may increase the female advantage, it doesn't appear to completely account for it.

Social Perception

A very different kind of perception is involved in using the information from other people's behaviors, especially while communicating. Although we usually think of communication as involving language, we also know that there are many other cues that do not involve words. Tone of voice, posture or attitude, and gestures are examples. It has been reported that people's ratings of an individual as hostile or friendly, sincere or not, and so on, are influenced much more by nonverbal cues than by what the person says (Argyle, Salter, Nicholson, Williams, and Burgess, 1970).

It is generally believed that women are more attuned to cues such as facial expression or tone of voice, and this opinion appears to be supported by objective studies. In a survey of over 50 published studies, Judith Hall (1984) reported that more than 80 percent of the studies found women to be better than men at reading such signs, though not all sex differences reached a statistically significant level.

The differences were particularly striking for the use of visual cues such as body movement and facial expression. We might expect that the more accurate processing of facial expression and other "body language" would have been more valuable to women than to men in our evolutionary past. It would have enabled them to avoid conflict and injury in a male-dominated world. It might also be helpful in the care of children. A mother's ability to read from its facial or body expression the state of a child who is unable to say what is wrong, would have enhanced her children's survival, and, consequently, the likelihood that such an ability would be transmitted to her offspring.

Summary

Women appear to be more sensitive to external stimuli than men in all modalities except vision, where the picture is more mixed. Despite the superior ability men possess in imaginal rotation, including 3-dimensional rotation, the appreciation of depth, at least within personal space, may be better in women. Women also are superior on an ability called "perceptual speed," in which rapid identity comparisons must be made. Finally, women appear to be consistently better than men at reading facial and body expressions.

Further Readings

Argyle M., Salter V., Nicholson H., Williams M. & Burgess P. (1970) The communication of inferior and superior attitudes by verbal and non-verbal signals. *British Journal of Social and Clinical Psychology*, 9, 222–231.

Burg A. (1966) Visual acuity as measured by dynamic and static tests. *Journal of Applied Psychology*, 50, 460–466.

Burg A. (1968) Lateral visual field as related to age and sex. *Journal of Applied Psychology*, 52, 10–15.

Dewar R. (1967) Sex differences in the magnitude and practice decrement of the Müller-Lyer illusion. *Psychonomic Science*, 9, 345–346.

Ekstrom R.B., French J.W., Harman H.H. & Dermen D. (1976) *Kit of factor-referenced cognitive tests*. Princeton, NJ: Educational Testing Service.

Ghent-Braine L. (1961) Developmental changes in tactual thresholds on dominant and nondominant sides. *Journal of Comparative & Physiological Psychology*, 54, 670–673.

Ginsburg N., Jurenovskis M., & Jamieson J. (1982) Sex differences in critical flicker frequency. *Perceptual & Motor Skills*, 54, 1079–1082.

Gwiazda J., Bauer J. & Held R. (1989) Binocular function in human infants: correlation of stereoptic and fusion-rivalry discriminations. *Journal of Pediatric Ophthalmology and Strabismus*, 26, 128–132.

Hall J. (1984) *Nonverbal sex differences*. Baltimore: Johns Hopkins.

Joseph, J.E. Personal Communication to the author by e mail, 9 Dec 1996. (Women fused random-dot numbers more quickly)

Julesz B. (1964) Binocular depth perception without familiarity cues. *Science*, 145, 356–362.

Majeres R.L. (1983) Sex differences in Symbol-Digit substitution and speeded matching. *Intelligence*, 7, 313–327.

McGuinness D. (1972) Hearing: individual differences in perceiving. *Perception*, 1, 465–473.

Peterson R.C. (1993) *A sex difference in stereoscopic depth perception*. Unpublished Master's thesis, Department of Psychology, University of Western Ontario.

Smith A. (1967) Consistent sex differences in a specific (decoding) test performance. *Educational & Psychological Measurement*, 27, 1077–1083.

Velle W. (1987) Sex differences in sensory functions. *Perspectives in Biology & Medicine*, 30, 490–522.

Wechsler D. (1958) *The measurement and appraisal of adult intelligence*. Baltimore: Williams & Wilkins, p. 146.

Weinstein S. & Sersen E.A. (1961) Tactual sensitivity as a function of handedness and laterality. *Journal of Comparative & Physiological Psychology*, 54, 665–669.

Witkin H.A. (1967) A cognitive style approach to cross-cultural research. *International Journal of Psychology*, 2, 233–250.

8
Verbal Abilities

The impression many people have, that women generally possess better skill with words than men do, probably arises from differences apparent between very young girls and boys. When speaking first begins, girls on average articulate earlier and better than boys, and produce longer sentences (Maccoby, 1966). To the extent that they speak earlier, they also have larger working vocabularies at very young ages. Girls speak more grammatically as well, and there is universal agreement that girls are better spellers than boys are—again on average. Reading is also typically superior in girls. Finally, they are more "fluent" on tests requiring them to generate words with particular limitations on them (such as words containing particular letters), though they are not necessarily more fluent in narrative output.

Because girls develop many other behaviors and skills earlier than boys do, we need to consider whether some of these female advantages disappear or diminish later in life. How many of the differences in verbal skills survive into adolescence or adult life? The answer is, probably only fluency, spelling, and grammatical usage. Verbal intelligence as measured on standard tests, including vocabulary items (defining the meaning of words), is not higher in adult women. Keep in mind, however, that the tendency of intelligence-test constructors to eliminate tests showing large sex differences may have resulted in the omission of some verbal tests on which women do better than men.

The Differential Aptitude Test (DAT) contains measures of a number of abilities thought to be important in school performance. It has been standardized on thousands of young people chosen so as to be representative of the U.S. population as a whole. We can get a fair idea of how young men and women differ on such abilities by restricting ourselves to the results for grade 12, which would represent the late teens. It is clear that at this age girls still have superior grammar and spelling skills (Hyde and Linn, 1988). In fact, the female advantage on spelling is if anything stronger in grade 12 than in grade 8 (Feingold, 1988). We can probably all think of otherwise bright people who are extremely poor spellers, and, while the occasional poor speller is a woman, more often he is a man. On a language test that asks people to identify ungrammatical sentences or parts of sentences, young women also scored significantly higher than young men.

Verbal fluency is another ability that continues to show an advantage for women in adulthood. To many people "fluency" implies an ease in producing coherent sentences, but in fact we have no evidence that women excel at this skill. Psychologists typically use the term "fluency" to refer to tasks in which subjects have to produce words or sentences with particular constraints on them, within a limited time period. For example, the test may limit the specific *letters* the words contain, such as requiring words starting with the letter "b" (big, brown, boss, etc.). Another meaning of verbal fluency is the capacity to produce words belonging to a particular class of objects, such as listing as many pieces of furniture as possible within a given time. These kinds of tests are sometimes called tasks of "divergent" production, meaning that a variety of answers is acceptable, in contrast to tests on which there is only one correct answer.

On verbal fluency tasks where either the beginning and/or ending letter of a word is specified (be it of a list of words or of words in sentences), when a difference is found, women tend to do better. However, there is a great deal of overlap between men and women, the differences favoring women are not found in every study, and in technical terms we would say that the *effect size* is small. Women's better fluency might be explained by better brain representation for the individual sounds of parts of words (called *phonemes*), which would fit well with the findings on young girls' better articulation and with women's continued superior spelling ability as adults.

The degree of fluency in generating words belonging to a nonphonemic category, sometimes called "ideational fluency" seems to depend on the kind of category asked for. When asked for lists of "things round" or "things metal," men may get better scores (Harshman, Hampson, and Berenbaum, 1983)); whereas if the category is "things red" or "things white," females do better (Kimura, 1994). It is possible that the female superiority on the latter task is related to women's superior ability to access color categories. We know that girls name a series of color patches or circles faster than do boys throughout elementary and early high school (Denckla and Rudel, 1974; DuBois, 1939; Ligon, 1932). Some studies report that girls also read color names, presented in black-and white-text, faster than boys do but this finding is less reliable than the difference in color naming. We have found a similar female advantage in color naming speed in university undergraduates, as have others (Brown, 1915; Stroop, 1935).

If we ask whether the reading of words is faster in women when the words do not name colors, the answer appears to be no. Women are not significantly faster than men when reading aloud either a paragraph of text as quickly as possible, or just the list of unrelated words contained in the same text (Ponton, 1987). One study showing faster color naming in girls as early as age five (Denckla and Rudel, 1974) reported that when these same children named numbers or letters, there was no significant sex difference.

That the female advantage on speeded naming of colors may be related to a special color factor in women is suggested by a study in our lab. We asked men and women to name not only a series of colors but also simple geometric forms in the same page arrangement as the colors (figure 8.1) (Woodworth and Wells, 1911). In one study we did, women were faster at naming forms as well as colors (Kimura, Saucier, and Matuk, 1996); but in two attempts at repeating this finding, we found no difference between the sexes on forms, but did find a consistent female advantage on colors. Nor was this advantage due simply to an ability to talk faster; on measures of articulation speed such as repeating tongue twisters and rapid counting, women were not significantly faster than men. More to the point, the rate of articulation did not account for the faster color naming. It seems therefore that women have either readier access to verbal *labels* for colors, or some special ability to identify color patches readily.

Figure 8.1
Geometric forms used to measure speed in naming forms. There is no reliable advantage for women on this test, in contrast to naming color squares in a similar arrangement. (From Woodworth & Wells, 1911.)

If instead of these fairly specific kinds of abilities involving words, we ask whether women are better on verbal tasks overall, the best source for such information is the verbal section of intelligence tests. The creators of intelligence tests carefully chose large numbers of people to be representative of the population as a whole in terms of occupational background, race, sex, and so on. The verbal half of the Wechsler Adult Intelligence Scale (WAIS) includes measures labeled: Information (general knowledge of the world), Comprehension (verbalizing responses to social conundrums), Arithmetic, Digit Span (how many digits can be repeated back correctly), Similarities (saying how two named things are alike), and Vocabulary (defining words). All of these subtests except Digit Span require some level of semantic and abstract ability, and none rely merely on articulatory skill. On this Verbal Scale, which gives a combined score for all the tests mentioned, men have shown a small advantage in almost every standardized sample since the inception of the WAIS. In originally devising his IQ test, Wechsler omitted tests that yielded large sex differences (such as mental rotation tests), the intent being to equate IQ scores obtained by men and women. So it is despite this aim that there is a slight edge for men on the Verbal IQ, indicating that, popular beliefs and claims to the contrary, women are not more verbally intelligent than men (Halpern, 1992; Hyde and Linn, 1988; Jensen, and Reynolds, 1983).

Verbal Memory

On another quite different ability related to the use of words, however, women are consistently better. This is in the recall of words or of material that can readily be mediated verbally. The advantage appears at all ages so far tested, from young (Duggan, 1950; McGuinness, Olson, and Chapman, 1990) to old (Bleecker, Bolla-Wilson, and Meyers, 1988; Bromley, 1958), and regardless of whether the material is simple recall of a list of unrelated words or digits, or memory for the content of a paragraph. This may help to explain why a man and a woman who have shared a particular experience sometimes differ in what they recall, particularly about what was said. On average, we would expect women to have more accurate recall.

So, for example, if we look at those subtests of the Wechsler Intelligence Scale for Children (WISC) that tap memory (such as Digit Span), we find that girls do better than boys, whereas on other verbal factors, if anything boys do better (Jensen and Reynolds, 1983). We see a similar effect in the results of young men and women taking medical school admission tests: women do better on a test called Learning Facts, which is a verbal memory task (Stumpf and Jackson, 1994). Adult women also learn a list of words read aloud more readily than men do (Kramer, Delis, and Daniel, 1988), and the sex difference is evident right from the first of several trials. It also appears that women tend to cluster the words they report in meaningful categories, whereas men tend to report them in the order given.

The difference between men and women in verbal memory may be stronger when recall of a meaningful text or paragraph is required, and this sex difference emerges across cultures. Thus in both black and white populations in a South African study (Owen and Lynn, 1993) and in a comparative American and Japanese study (Mann, Sasanuma, Sakuma and Masaki, 1990), women had better recall of a paragraph than their male compatriots. In the latter study there was no sex difference in recall of irregular nonsense shapes, suggesting that when items cannot be named, there may be no female advantage.

The question whether the memory advantage in females is really limited to verbal material—that is, to situations in which names or labels can be employed—is not entirely resolved. Several studies have suggested that females may have better recall of items other than words. Jensen reported that girls were better at, among other things, recall of a tapping sequence that involved remembering the order in which a series of four blocks was touched. However, one could argue that some people use an implicit labeling system to solve this problem, and that this technique might provide an advantage for as few as four items. If they imagine the blocks as 1–2–3–4, such verbalizing of the numbers might be particularly helpful to females. On a more complex block span task, in which the blocks are not in a tidy row, and the series is much longer, women are not better than men (Capitani, Laiacona, and Ciceri, 1991; Grossi, Orsini, Monetti, and DeMichele, 1979). If anything, the reverse is the case.

Better scores by women than men have also been reported on a "visual" memory task (Harshman et al., 1983). Using a similar task, Galea and the author (1993) also found a female superiority, at least for recognizing items after a short delay. However, in both these studies, subjects were presented with an array of line drawings of familiar objects which could be readily named; they subsequently received a second sheet of drawings and were asked to cross out those that had been presented on the first sheet (figure 8.2). Although there was no requirement that the objects be named, we can't rule out the possibility that unconscious naming may have contributed to women's higher scores. Similarly, in a study of high-school teenagers, in which items were presented one at a time, girls recalled by name a greater number of common objects (and also more words) than boys did (Duggan, 1950). Not only were the objects namable, but the name was actually given while the object was presented, again raising the possibility that labeling the items may have conferred an advantage on females.

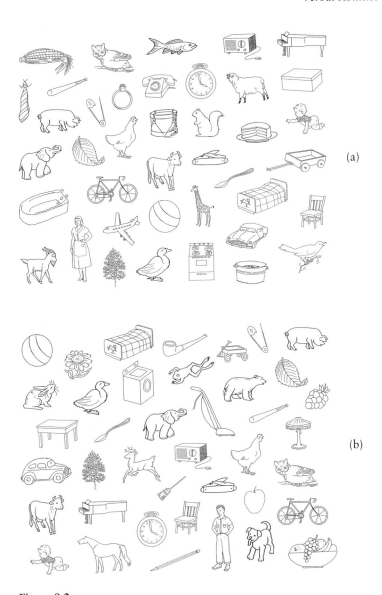

Figure 8.2
A reduced-size version of a test for item memory. The originals were 11" × 14".
(a) Subjects were given this sheet of 40 items and allowed to study it for one
minute. (b) The second sheet of 40 items (containing 20 items from the first sheet)
was presented for recall. The subjects were asked to cross out all items that could
be recalled from the first sheet. (From Galea and Kimura, 1993.)

Women possibly have the capacity to make the connection from object to object-name more readily than men, which would make later recall easier. In support of this idea, one study found that young girls were consistently better than young boys at recalling pictures by name, but when subjects were required to draw the pictures, there was no difference in recall between boys and girls (McGuinness, Olson, and Chapman, 1990). One problem in interpreting this finding is that boys may simply be better at drawing than girls are, although the authors attempted to avoid this difficulty by stressing that the drawings need not be good, just recognizable. Along similar lines, an Australian study (Ivison, 1977) found that women were slightly better at remembering a list of pairs of words presented together (e.g., cow-tree), but that men were slightly better on a task in which they had to draw from memory some simple nonverbal designs.

The obvious inference that women are better at all memory tasks involving words, or only at memory tasks which allow the use of words, may be premature. In the Duggan study on teenagers mentioned earlier, although girls were better at object and word memory, boys recalled more two-digit numbers than girls did. Since the numbers were spoken and so had a strong verbal component, this finding is remarkable, indicating that the numerical association may have been enough to produce a reversal of the usual sex difference. In contrast, some studies have shown that the recall span for single digits (as in a Digit Span test) is, if anything, better in women (Kail and Siegel, 1978).

Studies showing that women are better at associating names with faces raise similar questions concerning the degree to which this superiority reflects specifically *verbal* memory (Witryol and Kaess, 1957). It could be that women also process face identities better than men do, but until we have some evidence for this possibility, independent of the use of names, it remains an open question.

Researchers sometimes make a distinction between *incidental* and *intentional* memory. Incidental memory refers to the ability to recall stimuli or events that one was not specifically instructed to recall. Usually, some other response has to be made to the stimulus during presentation, to keep subjects from suspecting that their memory will be tested. For example, a list of words may be presented one at a time, and the subject asked to classify each item as referring to either "living" or "nonliving" things. Afterwards, the experimenter will unexpectedly ask for recall of the words. Intentional memory, in contrast, refers to deliberate attempts to remember material while it is being presented. In this case, a list of words might be presented with instructions to remember as many as possible for later recall.

There seems to be a general impression that women are better at recalling details or characteristics of events under conditions of incidental learning. However, Karen Chipman (Chipman and Kimura, in press) in my lab has investigated this question and has failed to find support for the supposition. She showed pictures of complex scenes (figure 8.3) and asked subjects to generate a title appropriate to each picture. With their own titles as reminders, subjects subsequently were asked questions about the details of the pictures. Contrary to what one might expect if they have better incidental memory, women were not better able than men to reply to such followup questions.

In fact, it again appears that nearly all tasks at which women are claimed to have better incidental memory used words or readily verbalized stimuli, such as familiar objects (e.g., McGuinness et al., 1990; Meinke, 1969). Since we know that women have better "intentional" verbal memory than men, the question arose whether the better incidental memory could be explained on that basis, without invoking any special incidental memory advantage. To answer that question, we gave subjects incidental memory tasks using concrete nouns (i.e., nouns referring to a tangible object) and namable line drawings; the distracting task was to quickly sketch a related object. We also gave the same subjects a different intentional verbal memory task, consisting of a list of words for recall. Women were better at all of these tasks than men were. However, when we corrected for their better *intentional* verbal memory, women's advantage for the *incidental* memory tasks disappeared. This suggests that there was no special female advantage for incidental memory.

It is interesting to speculate about how women's better verbal memory might have come about, in the context of the evolutionary scenario we discussed earlier. It has often been pointed out that mothers spend more time talking to their infants than do fathers, but this kind of verbal output does not put any demands on memory.

Figure 8.3
Example of one complex picture presented for a test of nonverbal incidental memory. The questions for this particular picture were: (1) Were there any flags on the ferry? (If answered correctly) How many flags? (2) In which direction was the ferry travelling, relative to yourself? (Chipman and Kimura, in press.)

One possibility is that women's greater use of landmarks for navigating puts heavier demands on verbal memory than does a geometric strategy. Most landmarks can be labeled in some way, and women do verbally recall more of such landmarks after learning a route than men do. Recalling landmarks by name would make it easier to find them again; and would also make it easier to communicate the location of important resources like food and fuel. Given that men use landmarks less often, there would be less advantage in having a memory system that records them.

Another possibility is that activities like cooking, sewing, basket making, and so forth, may require more ordering of movements into a preset sequence than do activities like throwing or tracking of game. Being able to verbalize the order in which household tasks must be done might have been adaptive.

Whatever the basis for the female advantage on verbal memory it is one of the strongest sex differences favoring women.

Summary

Many people have the impression that women possess better verbal skills than men do. In adulthood, however, women do not have larger vocabularies or higher verbal intelligence than men, though they do appear to be better spellers and to have slightly better "fluency" in the narrow sense of generating words that begin or end with specified letters.

On tasks of verbal memory, women perform consistently better than men. This is true for recalling both unrelated lists of words and more meaningful material. It may be that the superior memory for objects or items which women also show on certain tests is related to the fact that such items are readily named.

Some studies claim that women have better "incidental" recall than men do, but our own research suggests that this may be reducible to their superior intentional verbal memory.

Further Reading

Bleecker M.L., Bolla-Wilson K. & Meyers D.A. (1988) Age-related sex differences in verbal memory. *Journal of Clinical Psychology*, 44, 403–411.

Bromley D.B. (1958) Some effects of age on short term learning and remembering. *Journal of Gerontology*, 13, 398–406.

Brown W. (1915) Practice in associating color-names with colors. *Psychological Review*, 22, 45–55.

Capitani E., Laiacona M. & Ciceri E. (1991) Sex differences in spatial memory: a reanalysis of block tapping long-term memory according to the short-term memory level. *Italian Journal of Neurological Science*, 12, 461–466.

Chipman K. & Kimura D. (in press) An investigation of sex differences in incidental memory for verbal and pictorial material. *Learning & Individual Differences*.

Denckla M.B. & Rudel R. (1974) Rapid "automatized" naming of pictured objects, colors, letters and numbers by normal children. *Cortex*, 10, 186–202.

DuBois P.H. (1939) The sex difference on the color naming test. *American Journal of Psychology*, 52, 380–382.

Duggan L. (1950) An experiment on immediate recall in secondary school children. *British Journal of Psychology*, 40, 149–154.

Feingold A. (1988) Cognitive gender differences are disappearing. *American Psychologist*, 43, 95–103.

Galea L.A.M. & Kimura D. (1993) Sex differences in route-learning. *Personality & Individual Differences*, 14, 53–65.

Grossi D., Orsini A., Monetti C. & DeMichele G. (1979) Sex differences in children's spatial and verbal memory span. *Cortex*, 15, 667–670.

Halpern D.F. (1992) *Sex differences in cognitive abilities* (2nd edition). Hillsdale N.J.: Lawrence Erlbaum Associates.

Harshman R., Hampson E. & Berenbaum S. (1983) Individual differences in cognitive abilities and brain organization, Part I: Sex and handedness differences in ability. *Canadian Journal of Psychology*, 37, 144–192.

Hyde J.S. & Linn M.C. (1988) Gender differences in verbal ability: a meta-analysis. *Psychological Bulletin*, 104, 53–69.

Ivison D.J. (1977) The Wechsler Memory Scale: preliminary findings toward an Australian standardisation. *Australian Psychologist*, 12, 303–312.

Jensen A.R. & Reynolds C.R. (1983) Sex differences on the WISC-R. *Personality & Individual Differences*, 4, 223–226.

Kail R.V. & Siegel A.W. (1978) Sex and hemispheric differences in the recall of verbal and spatial information. *Cortex*, 14, 557–563.

Kimura D. (1994) Body asymmetry and intellectual pattern. *Personality & Individual Differences*, 17, 53–60.

Kimura D., Saucier D.M. & Matuk R. (1996) Women name both colors and forms faster than men. *Society for Neuroscience Abstracts*, 22, 1860 (Abstract).

Kramer J.H., Delis D.C. & Daniel M. (1988) Sex differences in verbal learning. *Journal of Clinical Psychology*, 44, 907–915.

Ligon E.M. (1932) A genetic study of color naming and word reading. *American Journal of Psychology*, 44, 103–122.

Maccoby E.E. (1966) *The development of sex differences*. Stanford: Stanford University Press.

Mann V.A., Sasanuma S., Sakuma N. & Masaki S. (1990) Sex differences in cognitive abilities: a cross-cultural perspective. *Neuropsychologia*, 28, 1063–1077.

McGuinness D., Olson A. & Chapman J. (1990) Sex differences in incidental recall for words and pictures. *Learning & Individual Differences*, 2, 263–285.

Meinke D.L. (1969) Stimulus properties, sex of subjects, and their effects upon incidental and intentional learning. *Proceedings of the 77th Annual Convention of the American Psychological Association*, 4, 79–80.

Owen K. & Lynn R. (1993) Sex differences in primary cognitive abilities among blacks, Indians and whites in South Africa. *Journal of Biosocial Science*, 25, 557–560.

Ponton C.W. (1987) Enhanced articulatory speed in ambidexters. *Neuropsychologia*, *25*, 305–311.

Stroop J.R. (1935) Studies of interference in serial verbal reactions. *Journal of Experimental Psychology*, *18*, 643–662.

Stumpf H. & Jackson D.N. (1994) Gender-related differences in cognitive abilities: evidence from a medical school admissions program. *Personality & Individual Differences*, *17*, 335–344.

Wechsler D. (1958) *The measurement and appraisal of adult intelligence*. Baltimore: Williams & Wilkins, pp. 145–147.

Witryol S.L. & Kaess W.A. (1957) Sex differences in social memory tasks. *Journal of Abnormal & Social Psychology*, *54*, 343–346.

Woodworth R.S. & Wells F.L. (1911) Association tests. *Psychological Monographs*, *13*, 1–85.

9

Hormonal Mechanisms

In chapter 3 we outlined the important role of sex hormones in organizing a variety of sexually dimorphic behaviors, including reproductive behavior, aggressive behavior, and rough-and-tumble play. Some interesting research on rodents suggests that the difference in spatial ability between males and females may also stem largely from different hormonal exposure early in life.

Male rats generally learn spatial mazes of the kind depicted in figure 9.1—the radial maze—more quickly and with fewer errors than female rats do. In this type of maze the rat's task is to find out which arms regularly contain food at the end of them. This cannot be determined from the central starting point. Since the maze is open at the top, the rat can see outside it. Some researchers have suggested that the male superiority on such spatial maze tasks is related to the species' evolutionary history, in that males had to travel longer distances in order to find receptive females. This explanation attributes their superiority in navigation to their polygynous nature. Support for the idea comes from another kind of rodent, the vole, in which a sex difference in spatial learning is found only in polygynous species. No sex difference appears in a closely related monogamous species, whose males do not wander (Gaulin, Fitzgerald, and Wartell, 1990).

Male and female rats also appear to employ different cues in learning a maze. In a laboratory situation, male rats seem to need information about the shape and angles of the room (i.e., geometric cues) to find the food. If the maze is surrounded by a high circular curtain, so that geometric cues are not available, males make more errors. Since females prefer to use objects in the room (landmarks) to find their way, they are not bothered by curtaining off the geometric cues as long as items like a

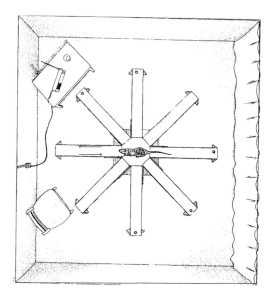

Figure 9.1
Radial arm maze. The rat learns which of the arms consistently contain food. The experimenter notes how many errors are made, and how many trials are required to achieve a criterion level. The items in the room outside the maze are considered "landmarks." (After Olton, 1977. Modified from the original, reproduced by permission of the artist, A. Iselin.)

picture or a table are visible. If the landmarks are moved, female rats make more errors, but when no landmarks are available, they can solve the maze with geometric cues.

Christina Williams and her co-workers (Williams, Barnett, and Meck, 1990) investigated the contribution of early exposure to sex hormones, to these different ways of navigating through mazes. She removed the effect of androgens in the males by castrating them at birth, and injected the females with estrogen (which has masculinizing effects—see chapter 3) right after birth. When tested on the radial arm maze as adults, the castrated males behaved like normal females; that is, they had a preference for landmark cues. The hormone-treated females behaved like normal males—they used geometric cues. This and other studies indicate very clearly that the rodent sex differences in spatial ability are determined by early exposure to sex hormones.

Precisely how sex hormones such as testosterone and estrogen act in the brain to produce behavioral, including cognitive, changes is currently the subject of much research, most of it using the rat as a model. It is generally agreed that androgens and estrogens act by binding to their specific receptors within cells. This, in turn, allows for the "transcription" of DNA to enable gene expression in specific ways (Becker & Breedlove, 1992), which are different for the two types of hormones. The locations of such receptors in the brain is one major determinant of what behaviors will be affected by the hormones. For example, concentrations of sex hormone receptors are found in the hypothalamus, the hippocampus, and parts of the cerebral cortex. These areas are structurally different in males and females, and the structural differences are known to be determined by the action of sex hormones early in life.

A recent study on the human brain looked at concentrations of estradiol and testosterone in postmortem samples of women's brains (Bixo, Backstrom, Winblad, and Andersson, 1995). As expected, the highest concentrations were found in certain parts of the hypothalamus, which is a critical area for sexual differentiation. However, until male brains are examined for comparison, the significance of differing hormone levels across various human brain regions remains undetermined.

Organization of Spatial Ability in Humans

In humans, as in nonhumans, there are peak periods when the levels of testosterone are much higher in males than in females. The first occurs during the prenatal period from approximately eight to twenty-four weeks. There is another period of peak testosterone right after birth until about five months of age (Michael and Zumpe, 1998). It seems quite possible that these times may correspond to the prenatal and postnatal "organizational" periods in other mammals; that is, those times when the brain is most sensitive to hormonal changes. Testosterone peaks again in males at the time of puberty.

In people we can't of course deliberately change the hormonal environment in order to investigate cognitive mechanisms. However, a number of hormone anomalies that occur spontaneously in people can help us understand how things work. One of these is the *androgen insensitivity syndrome*, in which XY individuals have testes (hidden in the abdominal cavity), and produce androgens; the body's cells, however, do not have functioning androgen receptors, and so are not affected by the androgens (chapter 3). These "girls," for such they seem to be, appear to have a cognitive makeup similar to XX girls; but since they are reared as females, it is difficult to disentangle the relative contributions of the genetic/hormonal and the environmental factors.

Another kind of hormone anomaly found in males is called by the complicated name of *idiopathic hypogonadotrophic hypogonadism* (IHH). These men have a lifelong deficiency in the hypothalamic gonadotrophic hormone which regulates production and release of sex hormones. Consequently they have abnormally low levels of testosterone and small genitals. The condition is often not diagnosed until puberty. Their spatial ability as young men is worse than that of normal males, and also of males who have suffered a testosterone deficiency later in life. This suggests that it is not current levels alone that are affecting abilities, but early deficiencies as well (Hier and Crowley, 1982). However, since the condition is usually of long standing by the time of diagnosis, one cannot to be certain that it is only the early deficiency of androgens which is the critical factor.

For this reason, the cognitive pattern in another hormone syndrome is of great interest. People with *congenital adrenal hyperplasia* (CAH), have excess levels of androgens due to overproduction by the adrenals of a testosterone-like androgen, *androstenedione*. The condition can occur in both males and females. In female infants it generally results in somewhat masculinized genitals, which is the first clue that something is wrong. This is usually remedied by surgery in the first year, and the flow of androgens is stopped by corrective hormone therapy. In the ideal case, then, the level of androgens is unusually high only before and for a short time after birth, so that any effects seen on behavior in later life may be attributed to the androgenic influences during that limited period.

Earlier studies on CAH girls seemed to suggest that their general intelligence was above average, but this has not been consistently confirmed. Instead, it appears that it may have been primarily girls from higher socioeconomic backgrounds who were brought for identification and treatment three or four decades ago, but that this is no longer the case. More recent studies, using sisters or other close female relatives as a comparison group, suggest that it is primarily spatial ability that is enhanced in CAH girls (Hampson, Rovet, and Altmann, 1998; Resnick, Berenbaum, Gottesmann, and Bouchard, 1986). The spatial tests on which CAH girls show enhanced ability include rotation tasks (see figure 5.1), visualization tests such as Paperfolding (figure 5.7), and disembedding tests such as Hidden Figures (figure 5.8). All of these are tests on which men usually get higher scores than women do. Less reliable differences are found on tests favoring women, such as verbal fluency and perceptual speed, so it seems that early exposure to androgens may or may not depress these abilities.

CAH boys are usually identified through general neonatal screening or when screened because another family member has CAH. Their heightened exposure to androgens apparently does not give them better spatial ability than normal boys. In fact, in one study, there was a tendency for CAH boys to be worse at spatial tasks than normal boys (Resnick et al., 1986), and in another, this effect was statistically significant (Hampson et al., 1998). So supernormal exposure to androgens in males may actually decrease some male-typical skills. Taken together, the data from males and females with CAH suggest that spatial ability may be best in those people with early androgen levels in the intermediate, or low-male, range.

This finding parallels the pattern identified in young men and women with normal early hormonal environments, in that the adult testosterone (T) level associated with optimal spatial ability is in the low male range. That is, women with higher testosterone levels have better spatial ability than those with lower levels, but in men it is those with lower T levels who get better scores (figure 9.2) (Gouchie and Kimura, 1991; Shute, Pellegrino, Hubert, and Reynolds, 1983). The optimal T level again seems to be in the low-normal male range. Note, however, that this finding is somewhat different from the results of the CAH studies, in that, when CAH individuals are tested, their hormone levels have been therapeutically returned to normal; thus the effects found can be attributed to *early* organizational androgen exposure. In the normal young men and women, we are relating cognitive functions to *current* hormone levels, and we cannot be certain that these reflect the early hormone environment. That

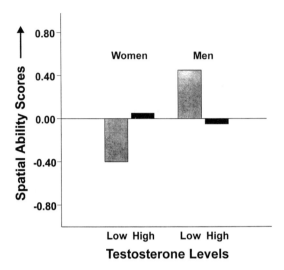

Figure 9.2
Relation between testosterone (T) levels and spatial ability in men and women. Zero represents the average of all four groups. Women with higher T levels have higher spatial scores than those with lower levels. The reverse is true in men. (After Gouchie and Kimura, 1991).

is, we don't know that adults with high T levels also had higher levels in early development.

Ideally, of course, we would like to know how hormone levels before or right after birth relate to the levels in adulthood, and also how such early hormone measures relate to cognitive tests in adulthood—a situation very difficult to achieve. We would have to measure hormone levels in a group of newborns, and then measure the cognitive function and hormone levels in the same people in their early twenties. No such study has yet been done. One study, however, did obtain information on testosterone levels in prenatal amniotic fluid and measured mental rotation when the children were seven years old (Grimshaw, Sitarenios and Finegan, 1995). The data were suggestive of a relation between T levels and rotation scores that resembled the adult pattern, but were not entirely convincing. Further studies of this kind are needed to establish more firmly the relation between *early* normal hormone levels and later cognitive pattern.

Sex differences in cognitive function, at least for some abilities, persist in older people whose hormones levels have dropped drastically. For example, women still have better verbal memory than men do well into their eighties (Bleecker, Bolla-Wilson, Agnew, and Meyers, 1988), whereas men at the same age still have superior spatial rotational ability (Willis and Schaie, 1988) and perform better than women do on the Water-Level task (see figure 5.10) (Robert and Tanguay, 1990). However, sex differences on the Rod-and-Frame test (figure 5.9) may not persist into old age (Robert and Tanguay, 1990; Schwartz and Karp, 1967). It may be that some cognitive abilities are more sensitive to ongoing changes in hormone levels than others are, but we have too little information on this topic to say more at present.

The collection of data relating hormone levels to cognitive function has been made much easier in recent years by the development of techniques for testing hormone levels in saliva. Instead of having blood extracted with a needle, subjects can spit into a bottle, a much more acceptable procedure for most people. Saliva, however, contains only what are called "unbound" or "free" hormones, unlike blood which also contains molecules bound to sex-hormone-binding-globulin (SHBG). Whether this fact limits the kinds of relationships we can uncover using saliva is still uncertain,[1] although increasing numbers of studies are showing reliable relationships between T levels in saliva and a variety of behavioral measures.

In our laboratory we have found that men's math reasoning and spatial scores show a similar relation to their T levels, that is, men with lower T levels get the highest scores (Gouchie and Kimura, 1991). In women, we have not found any relationship with math scores. Nor have we found any relation between T levels and performance on tests of perceptual speed, on which women get better scores. If the relation between T levels and math scores holds up in men, it will reinforce the suggestion that some of the differences in math reasoning ability across individuals is influenced by biological factors like hormone levels (Benbow, 1988).

When we measure existing sex hormones in individuals, by whatever method, and find a relation between such levels and scores on cognitive tests, we are engaging in what is called *correlational* research (see appendix)—that is, we can't necessarily claim that the hormone levels are the direct cause of the cognitive pattern. It might be, for example, that high testosterone levels in men interfere with the acquisition of certain cognitive skills because such men are more involved with sports or other activities than men with lower levels. Although this may seem unlikely, it is not an impossible explanation. To draw the best inferences from our results, therefore, we need to consider all available findings on the relation between sex hormones and behavior.

One helpful source of information is what happens when people are given sex hormones. Of course this would not be done just out of scientific curiosity about cognitive function, but usually for therapeutic reasons. Here again, we must be cautious, because the sample of people so treated may be different in some fundamental way from people who do not seek treatment. In one study, testosterone was administered to men in their sixties and seventies, who generally have much lower levels of T than younger men (Vermeulen, 1991). They were assessed on a number of intellectual functions just before going on T therapy and again approximately three months later; the results were compared to those of a similar group of men given placebo treatment at the same intervals (Janowsky, Oviatt and Orwall, 1994). Neither the subjects nor the experimenters were told who was receiving T and who was receiving placebo, a procedure called a "double blind" study.

When a test of an ability is taken twice, even at an interval of several months, subjects often improve at the second testing, even though test items are usually different. It is not clear why this happens, but it is a common finding, and is probably due to several factors (e.g., developing some useful strategies, and/or being more relaxed and familiar with the material). This phenomenon is one reason we use *control* groups of untreated people (such as the placebo group in this study), to help sort out the causes of changes in performance.

In this study, the only test on which there was a *different* change in the group receiving T therapy compared with the no-T group, was on a Block Design test (figure 9.3). That test requires the construction, from a set of blocks, of a design pictured on a card, and it is known to involve both spatial and complex motor activity. The men who received T therapy improved on the Block Design score, whereas those without T actually declined slightly (Janowsky et al., 1994). Unfortunately, since the study

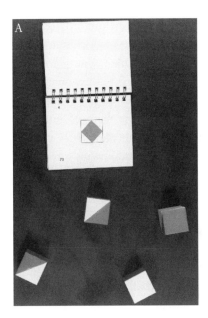

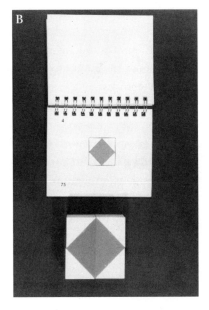

Figure 9.3
An example of a Block Design item. The diagram pictured on the card must be constructed from the blocks that are shown: (a) before assembly (b) after solution.

was not primarily concerned with the effects of T on cognitive function, none of the tests known to show large male advantages, such as mental rotation, were administered.

Why should raising T levels improve performance on a spatial constructional task, given that in young men, it is those with lower levels who do best on spatial tests? We can safely assume that the T levels in the older men were well below those of the younger men in previous studies, since T levels decline with age (though we can't always compare absolute levels directly, when one employs saliva and the other, blood assays). So it is possible that the hormone therapy simply raised the older men's T levels into the optimal or low-normal male range.

Another study in which sex hormones were administered also suggests that they can affect cognitive function in humans. This involved a group of women who were undergoing androgen therapy before having a sex change operation, and a group of men undergoing anti-androgen and estrogen therapy before having the opposite sex change (Van Goozen et al., 1995). There were also two control groups of men and women who were not undergoing treatment. All groups were tested on a variety of measures before and again three months after the start of hormone treatment (or for the control groups, simply once and again three months later). In addition to measures of mood and aggressiveness, tests given included a rotated figures test, a verbal reasoning test, and two tests of verbal fluency—one requiring subjects to generate words belonging to particular object categories, and the other to generate sentences in which the beginning letters of each of the words was specified.

On the rotated figures test, all groups except the male-to-female transsexuals (i.e., those undergoing anti-androgen therapy) improved on second testing; the latter actually showed a small decline. Recall that rotational tasks are those on which men typically excel. Improvement was slightly greater in the female-to-male transsexuals who underwent androgen therapy than in the other three groups. There was no change on verbal reasoning, an area in which there are usually no differences found between men and women.

On the verbal fluency tasks, the picture is rather unclear because performance actually declined in all groups, suggesting that the tests given to measure this function on the two occasions were not equivalent. However, female-to-male transsexuals (given androgen therapy) showed the largest drop in performance, yet this was the group which improved most on the rotation task. Recall that women generally perform better on fluency tasks involving the production of words or sentences with specified beginning letters.

So these findings suggest that female-to-male transsexuals given androgen therapy undergo a change in cognitive pattern in the masculine direction at least on some cognitive tasks. In contrast, male-to-female transsexuals undergoing anti-androgen or estrogen therapy may undergo a change in the feminine direction. These findings would fit with the idea that moderate increases in androgens enhance certain spatial skills (while perhaps depressing verbal fluency); whereas anti-androgen or estrogen therapy may depress spatial skills.

We need to consider whether similar effects would be seen in ordinary people who are not seeking to make a sex change. It is possible that women who want to become men are already different from ordinary women, perhaps because they had anomalous levels of exposure to androgens earlier in life. Such exposure might make it more likely that androgens will have an "activating" effect on them. Similarly, men who want to become women may in some way always have been different neurohormonally, which may also make them more susceptible to estrogen therapy. We don't have the answers to these questions yet, but the report that there are brain differences between transsexuals and normal controls of the same sex (Zhou, Hofman, Gooren, and Swaab, 1995) reinforces that possibility.

Natural Hormonal Fluctuations

As it turns out, the natural fluctuations in sex hormones experienced by healthy young adults also result in changes in cognitive pattern, and in ways that are consistent with the findings in the hormonal anomalies just described. Women undergo large variations in estrogen and progesterone levels across the natural menstrual cycle. Men experience changes in testosterone levels across the seasons, and within the course of the day. In both sexes, such hormonal changes are associated with predictable changes in cognitive strengths.

When we ask what brain changes are associated with these fluctuations in hormone levels, we again must look to animal, especially rat-based research to guide us. Natural fluctuations in hormones, and the changes induced by injection of hormones, may result in temporary alterations in some neurons. In the hippocampus, for example, high levels of estrogen increase dendritic spines and synapses onto dendrites (the receiving end of a nerve cell). Other hormone-induced changes in the brain include temporary variations in receptor numbers and fluctuations in the levels of certain neurotransmitters, the substances essential for communication between neurons (for review, see McEwen, 1991). It is reasonable to expect similar changes in humans, but as yet we have no direct confirmation in people.

In humans, the most thoroughly investigated influence of current or activational hormones on cognitive pattern has been the natural variations in estrogen levels across the menstrual cycle (figure 9.4). Because animal studies had suggested that the activating effects of hormones primarily affect sexually dimorphic behaviors (those that differentiate the sexes), Elizabeth Hampson (Hampson, 1990a,b; Hampson and Kimura, 1988) decided to measure changes across the menstrual cycle with tests that show sex differences in humans. She therefore used some spatial tests on which men typically score better, as well as tests of verbal fluency, fine manual skills, and perceptual speed, on which women score better.

Estrogen levels are high in the preovulatory peak in the late follicular phase in mid-cycle, and both estrogen and progesterone are high in the later midluteal period approximately five to ten days before menstruation. In contrast, levels of both hormones are very low at the onset of menstruation and for several days thereafter. Comparisons are therefore best made between the menstrual phase (three to five days after onset, to avoid complications from physical discomfort), and either the midluteal or preovulatory period. Because the latter phase is so short, it is especially difficult to pinpoint exactly without hormone assays.

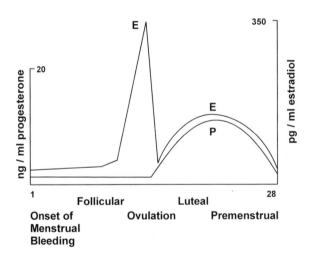

Figure 9.4
The menstrual cycle and associated hormonal variations. Estrogen levels are high in the pre-ovulatory and midluteal phases.

Not all studies show significant changes across the menstrual cycle. However, there have been problems of interpretation with some of this research, largely due to wide variation in the definition of the phase of the menstrual cycle. Although the length of the entire cycle varies from person to person, the interval between ovulation and the onset of the next menstrual period is less variable, typically twelve to fourteen days, regardless of the total length of the cycle. Hampson therefore defined the midluteal period by working backward five to ten days from the onset of the next menstruation. In contrast, studies that normalize the menstrual cycle across individuals by putting, for example, a 25- and 30-day cycle on the same scale actually becloud the relation between hormone levels and any behavioral function measured.

Hampson found that women tested at the high-estrogen phases of the cycle scored better on tests on which women generally perform better—verbal fluency, and fine motor tasks, for example—than women tested in the low estrogen/menstrual phase. The latter scored better on spatial tests, on which men typically excel, than women in the high-estrogen phase. These spatial tests included not only complex paper-and-pencil tasks (see chapter 5 for examples), but also a relatively simple task on which subjects had to adjust a line to the vertical against a tilted background (see figure 5.9).

A parallel to the hormonal effects in humans is seen in female rats, whose estrogen levels also vary across the estrus cycle. Their performance on a spatial water maze was worst during the high-estrogen phase of the cycle (Warren and Juraska, 1997).

One motor task that Hampson found was more efficiently executed in high-estrogen phases of the cycle was a manual sequence box (figure 9.5), in which subjects had to perform different hand postures in quick succession. We wanted to compare this motor task with another motor task on which males are superior, throwing accuracy (see chapter 4). We found, as expected, that the women's performance on the box task was better in the midluteal high-estrogen phase of the cycle, but there was absolutely no cycle difference in accuracy on the throwing task (Saucier and Kimura, 1998). This again emphasizes the specificity of effects, in that not all motor tasks are affected in the same way by hormonal fluctuations. It also points out that not all "masculine" tasks need be affected in the same way

MANUAL SEQUENCE BOX

Figure 9.5
The Manual Sequence Box. The subject is required to press the top button with the index finger, pull forward the vertical bar with all four fingers and press down on the bottom bar with the side of the thumb. (From Kimura, 1977.)

by hormonal fluctuations. Some, like throwing, may be insensitive to such fluctuations, though this does not rule out the possibility that they are organized early in life by androgenic influences. We know that in male rats rough-and-tumble play in adolescence requires only early organizing hormonal exposure to appear in adolescence; no later priming by hormones is necessary.

The fact that Hampson found opposite effects on the masculine and feminine tests she used makes it unlikely that the hormonal influences observed were due to general factors (such as alertness or fatigue) which might change across the menstrual cycle. Instead, it seems likely that the enhancement of female-favoring cognitive tasks during high estrogen phases is somehow related to the role of estrogen in facilitating other aspects of adult female behavior.

When the facts on menstrual cycle changes in cognition were first presented at a scientific meeting a few years ago, they received a great deal of attention from the media, and resulted in a storm of controversy. Many women commentators reportedly felt that the data would be used to reinforce stereotypes that supposedly pictured women as creatures of their moods; and some suspected there was a hidden agenda behind these studies. Unfortunately, as a result, most people missed the real significance of the research: that a substantial part of the cognitive difference between any two individuals may well be related to differing hormonal environments, either early in life or at the time of testing.

Ironically, we have known for some time that men's levels of testosterone vary, not only across seasons, but throughout the day. It seemed reasonable to expect that such hormonal fluctuations might affect cognitive patterns, as they do in women. Because hormonal changes evident in the blood stream or in saliva may not be followed immediately by brain and behavioral changes, we first examined the more stable hormonal states which persist through a season. Many male mammals, including humans, show seasonal variation in testosterone levels that are related to their breeding cycles. Testosterone levels are higher in the human male (at least in the northern hemisphere) in the fall than in the spring, with a consequent rise in sperm count in late fall. This would presumably facilitate the birth of the young in summer, a time when for our ancestors shelter was less critical and food more plentiful. Although such factors are less important in modern society, male physiology remains much the same as it was in our evolutionary pre-history.

We tested young men and women across two seasons on a variety of cognitive tests, some known to favor men, some known to favor women, and some known to show no difference between the sexes (see table 9.1) (Kimura and Hampson, 1994). The male-favoring tests in this study were all spatial; the female-favoring measures were either perceptual speed tests or ideational fluency tests; the neutral tests were tests of vocabulary and reasoning. Half the subjects were tested first in the spring, primarily in March, the others in the fall, primarily in October. Besides doing the cognitive tests, subjects also gave us saliva samples so that we could assay their testosterone levels. We tried to see as many of these people as possible again in the next season, six months later, but of course many were not available to return. However, the patterns of those retested were pretty much the same as those tested only in one season, except for the expected improvement from first to second session.

Men's T levels (as expected) were higher in the fall than the spring. Since

Table 9.1
Tests used in the study of seasonal changes in cognition

Neutral Tests
Vocabulary
Raven's Matrices
Inferences
"Feminine" Tests
Finding a's
Identical Pictures
Things red/white
"Masculine" Tests
Mental Rotation
Paper Folding
Hidden Figures

we had earlier found that men with higher levels of T scored worse on spatial tests than those with lower T, we predicted that spatial scores would be lower in fall than in spring. And that is exactly what happened (figure 9.6). Men's scores on the female-favoring and neutral tests did not change across seasons, and women showed no significant change on any of the types of tests across seasons. Thus the change in cognitive pattern in men was quite selective; only spatial scores changed, and they were higher in the spring than in the fall.[2] This again effectively rules out some general alertness or arousal factor as an explanation for the difference between seasons, because in that case other types of tests should be affected as well.

Recently, even variation in T levels throughout the day have been related to changes in spatial ability. Testosterone levels are highest in the early morning, and decline throughout the day. One would therefore expect that, if the brain changes occur within a reasonable time of the levels apparent in saliva, spatial ability would be better later in the day than in early morning, and this is what happened (Moffat and Hampson, 1996). It should be stressed that none of these hormonal fluctuations erase the difference between men and women in spatial scores, though of course it does mean that certain sex differences will be larger at some phases than at others.

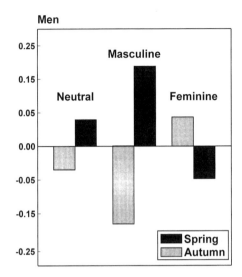

Figure 9.6
Seasonal performance by young men on various cognitive tasks. Zero represents
the mean for the two seasons, on each type of task. The only significant difference
between seasons is on so-called "masculine" (spatial) tasks.

So we have a fair amount of evidence that variations in estrogen across
women's menstrual cycle are related to changes in spatial, verbal fluency,
and articulatory-motor skills. In men, so far, variation in testosterone
levels across seasons or times of the day has been found to relate only to
changes in spatial ability. Do these changes in cognitive pattern within an
individual have any functional significance? Or are they merely ripples on
a basic system that depends on these hormones for, among other things,
a stable cognitive profile? We don't know the answer to that. It is possible
that changes in cognitive profile were actually adaptive in the hunter-
gatherer milieu in which these abilities evolved. For example, perhaps
having slightly better spatial ability in the spring than in the fall would
have resulted in more successful hunting when prey was scarce, or in
finding better campsites when it came time to move.

Could there be any advantage to variation in verbal fluency, or in
motor or perceptual speed skills during certain periods of the menstrual
cycle? Possibly some other hormone-induced change in behavior enhanced women's attractiveness during the preovulatory estrogen surge,

which would improve the chance of being impregnated. But it is also possible that there is no such effect, and that all behavioral changes, including cognitive and skill changes, represent merely an unimportant (but scientifically informative) by-product of the basic hormonal cycle.

Summary

There is good evidence in rodents that sex differences in spatial strategies are determined by the hormonal environment early in life. In humans, evidence for the contribution of the early sex hormone environment to adult spatial ability is more equivocal, because it is based on hormonal anomalies that are less time-limited in their effects. Nevertheless, the presence of heightened spatial ability in some females with congenital adrenal hyperplasia may be interpreted as an effect of their early exposure to excess androgens.

In normal young men and women, spatial ability is systematically related to testosterone (T) levels. Men with T levels in the low normal range, perform best at spatial and mathematical reasoning tasks. In women, those with higher T levels perform better on spatial tasks than those with lower levels. These facts suggest that the "optimal" level of T for spatial ability in humans is that of the normal male with lower levels. Testosterone levels in men vary across season and time of day, with higher levels in the autumn than in the spring, and in early morning than later in the day. Spatial ability in men is better in the spring and later in the day, findings that are consistent with other studies on T levels and spatial scores.

Women's cognitive pattern also varies according to phase of the menstrual cycle. In general, performance on tasks that favor women are enhanced in the high-estrogen phases of the cycle relative to the low-estrogen phases. However, spatial tasks, which favor men, show the opposite pattern, that is, they are performed better in the low-estrogen or menstrual phase.

That the cognitive changes accompanying these natural variations in levels of sex hormones are actually due to the hormone levels is suggested by a number of studies in which hormones have been administered to either older men and women or to persons about to undergo a sex change. The expected cognitive changes occurred.

Notes

1. The correlation between salivary testosterone levels and free testosterone in blood is generally found to be well over .80 (e.g., James & Baxendale, 1984), indicating that levels of free T in saliva correspond well to those in plasma.

2. This finding has often been misreported, e.g., "men performed more poorly on tests of spatial ability when tested in the spring" (Fausto-Sterling, 1992, p. 261).

Further Reading

Becker J.B. & Breedlove S.M. (1992) Introduction to behavioral endocrinology. In J.B. Becker, S.M. Breedlove & D. Crews (Eds.), *Behavioral endocrinology.* Cambridge, Mass: MIT Press, pp. 3–37.

Benbow C.P. (1988) Sex differences in mathematical reasoning ability in intellectually talented preadolescents: their nature, effects, and possible causes. *Behavioral & Brain Sciences*, 11, 169–232.

Bixo M., Bäckström T., Winblad B. & Andersson A. (1995) Estradiol and testosterone in specific regions of the human female brain in different endocrine states. *Journal of Steroid Biochemistry & Molecular Biology*, 55, 297–303.

Bleecker M.L., Bolla-Wilson K., Agnew J. & Meyers D.A. (1988) Age-related sex differences in verbal memory. *Journal of Clinical Psychology*, 44, 403–411.

Fausto-Sterling A. (1992) *Myths of gender.* New York: Basic Books (2nd edition).

Gaulin S.J.C., Fitzgerald R.W. & Wartell M.S. (1990) Sex differences in spatial ability and activity in two vole species. *Journal of Comparative Psychology*, 104, 88–93.

Gouchie C. & Kimura D. (1991) The relationship between testosterone levels and cognitive ability patterns. *Psychoneuroendocrinology*, 16, 323–334.

Grimshaw G.M., Sitarenios G. & Finegan J.K. (1995) Mental rotation at 7 years: relations with prenatal testosterone levels and spatial play experience. *Brain & Cognition*, 29, 85–100.

Hampson E. (1990a) Estrogen-related variations in human spatial and articulatory-motor skills. *Psychoneuroendocrinology*, 15, 97–111.

Hampson E. (1990b) Variations in sex-related cognitive abilities across the menstrual cycle. *Brain & Cognition*, 14, 26–43.

Hampson E. & Kimura D. (1988) Reciprocal effects of hormonal fluctuations on human motor and perceptual-spatial skills. *Behavioral Neuroscience*, 102, 456–459.

Hampson E., Rovet J.F. & Altmann D. (1998) Spatial reasoning in children with congenital adrenal hyperplasia due to 21-hydroxylase deficiency. *Developmental Neuropsychology*, 14, 299–320.

Hier D.B. & Crowley W.F. (1982) Spatial ability in androgen-deficient men. *New England Journal of Medicine, 306,* 1202–1205.

James V.H.T. & Baxendale P.M. (1984) Androgens in saliva. In G.F. Read, D. Riad-Fahmy, R.F. Walker & K. Griffiths (Eds.), *Immunoassays of steroids in saliva.* Proceedings of the 9th Tenovus Workshop. Cardiff: Alpha Omega Publishing, pp. 193–201.

Janowsky J.S., Oviatt S.K. & Orwoll E.S. (1994) Testosterone influences spatial cognition in older men. *Behavioral Neuroscience, 108,* 325–332.

Kimura D. (1977) Acquisition of a motor skill after left-hemisphere damage. *Brain, 100,* 527–542.

Kimura D. & Hampson E. (1994) Cognitive pattern in men and women is influenced by fluctuations in sex hormones. *Current Directions in Psychological Science, 3,* 57–61.

McEwen B.S. (1991) Our changing ideas about steroid effects on an ever-changing brain. *Seminars in the Neurosciences, 3,* 497–507.

Michael R.P. & Zumpe D. (1998) Developmental changes in behavior and in steroid uptake by the male and female macaque brain. *Developmental Neuropsychology, 14,* 233–260.

Moffat S.D. & Hampson E. (1996) A curvilinear relationship between testosterone and spatial cognition in humans: possible influence of hand preference. *Psychoneuroendocrinology, 21,* 323–337.

Olton D.S. (1977) Spatial memory. *Scientific American, 236,* 82–98.

Resnick S.M., Berenbaum S.A., Gottesmann I.I. & Bouchard T.J. (1986) Early hormonal influences on cognitive functioning in congenital adrenal hyperplasia. *Developmental Psychology, 22,* 191–198.

Robert M. & Tanguay M. (1990) Perception and representation of the Euclidean coordinates in mature and elderly men and women. *Experimental Aging Research, 16,* 123–131.

Saucier D.M. & Kimura D. (1998) Intrapersonal motor but not extrapersonal targeting skill is enhanced during the midluteal phase of the menstrual cycle. *Developmental Neuropsychology, 14,* 385–398.

Schwartz D.W. & Karp S.A. (1967) Field dependence in a geriatric population. *Perceptual & Motor Skills, 24,* 495–504.

Shute V.J., Pellegrino J.W., Hubert L. & Reynolds R.W. (1983) The relationship between androgen levels and human spatial abilities. *Bulletin of the Psychonomic Society, 21,* 465–468.

Van Goozen S.H.M., Cohen-Kettenis P.T., Gooren L.J.G., Frijda N.H. & Van de Poll N.E. (1995) Gender differences in behavior: activating effects of cross-sex hormones. *Psychoneuroendocrinology, 20,* 343–363.

Vermeulen A. (1991) Androgens in the aging male. *Journal of Clinical Endocrinology and Metabolism, 73,* 221–224.

Warren S.G. & Juraska J.M. (1997) Spatial and nonspatial learning across the rat estrous cycle. *Behavioral Neuroscience, 111,* 259–266.

Williams C.L., Barnett A.M. & Meck W.H. (1990) Organizational effects of early gonadal secretions on sexual differentiation in spatial memory. *Behavioral Neuroscience, 104,* 84–97.

Willis S.L. & Schaie K.W. (1988) Gender differences in spatial ability in old age: longitudinal and intervention findings. *Sex Roles, 18,* 189–203.

Zhou J-N., Hofman M.A., Gooren L.J.G. & Swaab D.F. (1995) A sex difference in the human brain and its relation to transsexuality. *Nature, 378,* 68–70.

10

Brain Mechanisms Studied in Normal Brains

Interest in the differences between men's and women's brains has existed for at least as long as the interest in cognitive differences. However, while we know a fair amount about sex differences in both brain and cognitive systems, we still have very little information about how the two may be related. That is, we still don't know much about how the different cognitive patterns of individuals are mediated by the brain.

The earlier chapters on sexual differentiation and hormonal mechanisms outlined what we know about the contribution of sex hormones to the structural and behavioral differences between the sexes. We found that most such differences could be related to the secondary hormonal effects of developing either testes or ovaries. There may, however, be sex differences that are mediated, not by hormonal differences, but directly, by other genes. Such genes may be on the X or Y chromosomes, or even on one of the *autosomes*, the other 22 pairs of chromosomes. Some preliminary studies in rodents suggest that genes other than those governing the formation of the testes may affect sex-typical brain features and behaviors, independent of the action of sex hormones (Maxson, 1997). So we need to keep in mind that, besides the genetically initiated hormone contributions, there may be other genetic factors affecting sex differences in brain and behavior.

Brain Size

The biggest structural brain difference between men and women is size. Men's brains are larger and heavier than women's by 10 to 15 percent. It used to be thought that this was simply accounted for by differences in body size; and in fact if one compares the *ratio* of brain-to-body size, there is no sex difference. Some, however, have argued that this does not tell the whole story, because this ratio decreases in humans as body size increases. Thus, larger women have smaller brain-to-body ratios than smaller women do. To control for this effect, Ankney (1992) compared men and women of the same body size and found that throughout the range of sizes, men's brains are about 100 grams heavier than women's. This means that, on average, a man and a woman of the same body size would still have a 100-gram difference in brain size. Recently, a group of Danish investigators found that the men in their sample had about four billion more cortical neurons (nerve cells) than did women, and this was not accounted for by differences in height (Pakkenberg and Gundersen, 1997).

The question then is, what might be the significance of such a difference? Ankney proposed that the extra brain weight in males is the basis for the large sex difference in spatial ability, reviewed in chapter 5. However, what little information we have suggests instead that brain size may relate to some more general intellectual function. The best of this research, which is fairly recent, uses methods that give us a picture of the brain in living people. This allows us to relate structural features of the brain to cognitive abilities measured in the same person. Across both men and women, the correlation of brain size with intelligence, as measured by standard IQ tests, is modest but statistically significant (Andreasen et al., 1993; Wickett, Vernon and Lee, 1994, 1996; Willerman, Rutledge, and Bigler, 1991). However, the same studies do not find that brain size is more highly related to Performance IQ than to Verbal IQ, yet the Performance IQ contains tests of visuoconstructional ability (e.g., Block Design, figure 9.3) that require some spatial analysis. So this finding argues against the idea that the extra brain weight in men contributes specifically to spatial ability.

Only two studies (Wickett et al., 1994, 1996) have so far looked at the relation between brain size and performance on particular spatial tests like Mental Rotation that show the largest sex differences (but are not part of standard IQ tests). One of these studies employed only women and the other, only men. The correlation of brain size with purely spatial tests like Mental Rotation was not statistically significant—that is, not different from zero—in either men or women. Yet in the same studies, brain size did correlate significantly with IQ subtests such as Digit Span and Arithmetic. So again, the findings did not support the idea that brain size relates to superior spatial skills. It would, however, be more convincing to know what happens in a *combined* sample of men and women, since the hypothesis that the extra brain weight relates to men's better spatial scores would predict a correlation that should appear across sexes. So far, no comparison of brain size and spatial scores has been made with a mixed-sex group.

Does the fact that brain size appears to correlate most highly with general intelligence mean that men should, on average, be brighter than women? The consensus in the past has been that there are no sex differences in intelligence. Recently, however, this view has been challenged by Richard Lynn (1994). He points out that the most widely used intelligence test, the Wechsler Adult Intelligence Scale, shows a small advantage for men, despite the fact that the most sex-sensitive components were already removed when the test was first devised. Other intelligence tests administered to adults show a similar pattern (Alexopoulos, 1996), and the difference gets larger when spatial tests are included. Lynn therefore estimated that men may actually have an "IQ" advantage of about four points. This rather controversial idea continues to be a source of much further research and discussion (for further debate on this topic see Lynn, 1998; Mackintosh, 1998; and others in the same journal issue).

Apart from overall brain size, there are many other structural features of the brain that appear sexually differentiated. Even in the absence of visible structural differences, much research suggests that the brains of men and women may function differently; that is, that particular anatomical regions may not take part in cognitive processes to the same degree or in the same way in the two sexes.

The Hypothalamus

Probably the most widely known region of the brain demonstrated to show sexual differentiation is the hypothalamus. No doubt this is due to the fact that it is an important site for mediating the different sexual behaviors of males and females. The hypothalamus is a clump of nuclei at the base of the brain, which we have known for a long time is important in general life functions such as eating, sleeping, reproduction, and so on. The effects of androgens in organizing male behaviors, which we described in chapter 3, are manifest in regions of the hypothalamus like the *preoptic area* (POA). A subregion of the preoptic area is larger in male rats than in females, and has been shown in Roger Gorski's lab to enlarge under early androgenic influence (Jacobson, Csernus, Shryne, and Gorski, 1981). This region has therefore been labeled the *sexually dimorphic nucleus of the preoptic area*, usually shortened to SDN-POA.

The human analogue of the SDN-POA is believed to be contained in the interstitial nuclei of the anterior hypothalamus or INAH, but precisely which of the four INAH nuclei are analogous to the SDN is a little unclear. Sex differences in the size of parts of INAH—with women showing smaller areas—have been reported from postmortem data by both Dutch and American researchers (Allen, Hines, Shryne, and Gorski, 1989; Swaab and Hofman, 1995).

What especially brought the attention of the world to this region of the hypothalamus, however, was the 1991 report by Simon LeVay that parts of INAH also differed between heterosexual and homosexual men. INAH-3, which is smaller in women than in men, was also smaller in LeVay's sample of homosexual men than in heterosexual men. A reasonable inference is that this size difference is in some way related to the sex of the partner one prefers. As LeVay himself pointed out, however, because the data are correlational, it is not yet clear what the determinants are. Does the size of the region in some way influence sexual orientation, or is the size difference a secondary consequence of other neural changes that influence sexual orientation? Or even, is there some other characteristic of LeVay's homosexual subjects that resulted in a smaller INAH-3?

In contrast to the INAH region, another hypothalamic nucleus, the suprachiasmatic nucleus, is larger in homosexual than in heterosexual men (Swaab and Hofman, 1995). This nucleus is concerned with regulating day-night, seasonal, and other biological rhythms, but again the significance of this difference to sexual orientation is unclear. In this connection it may be of interest that gay men in one undergraduate sample had a rise-and-retire pattern more like heterosexual women than like heterosexual men (Hall and Kimura, 1993). Women, on average, get up and go to bed earlier than men do, and the homosexual men tended to do the same.

Finally, there is an intriguing report on yet another hypothalamic structure involved in sexual behavior, the *bed nucleus of the stria terminalis* (BST), which is also larger in men than in women. One study found that the BST of genetically male transsexuals, who generally have the strong feeling that they have been born the wrong sex, was the same size as women's. This difference was apparently not due to the effects of the adult hormone changes which these men were undergoing (Zhou, Hofman, Gooren and Swaab, 1995).

The Hippocampal Complex

A region shown to be sexually dimorphic in some rodents, and which appears to serve spatial memory function, is the hippocampal complex. This structure includes the hippocampus and entorhinal cortex in the most medial part of the temporal lobe (figure 10.1). Removing parts of the rat hippocampal complex makes it difficult for the animals to solve spatial mazes of the kind depicted in figure 9.1. In addition, the hippocampus of bird species that store food is larger than in species that do not, suggesting that this structure is important to the ability to find previously stored food caches (Sherry, Vaccarino, Buckenham and Herz, 1989).

The hippocampal complex is also larger in male than in female rats, kangaroo rats, and polygynous species of voles. So a larger hippocampus appears to serve the functions of both food retrieval and the navigation of larger territories in polygynous males (see chapter 2) (Sherry, Jacobs, and Gaulin, 1992). The basis for the anatomical sex difference appears to be the early organizing influence of androgens (Roof and Havens, 1992).

To date, no analogous sex difference in human hippocampal size has been reported. One study on children, using brain imaging, reported no difference (Lucas, Lombardino, Roper and Leonard, 1996). If it turns out that there is no sex difference in the size of the human hippocampal complex, this may be related to a number of factors. For one thing, in

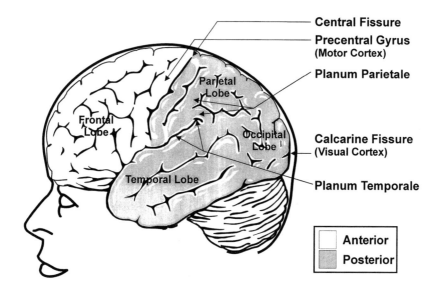

Figure 10.1
A view of the brain from the left side of the head. The planum temporale is visible only when the temporal lobe is pulled downwards to expose its top surface.

humans the hippocampal region appears to serve more generalized memory function, rather than specifically spatial memory (Milner, 1968). Remember also that human females have, if anything, better memory for location of objects—at least when they are part of an array—than men do (chapter 5). So we would be hard pressed to predict in humans which sex should have the larger hippocampus.

Interhemispheric Connections

Some of the earliest, albeit highly contested, reports of sex differences in the human brain, deal with variations in the *commissural* systems that connect the left and right hemispheres. In 1982 Christine DeLacoste and Ralph Holloway reported in *Science* that in women the posterior part of the corpus callosum (the major connection between the hemispheres) was larger and more bulbously shaped than in men. They discovered this by cutting through the corpus callosum in postmortem brains and measuring the cross-sectional area (figure 10.2).

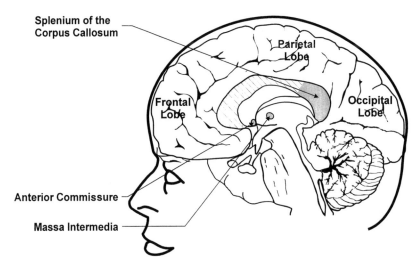

Figure 10.2
A view of the brain, through the midline of the head showing the corpus callosum, anterior commissure, and massa intermedia. In some studies, the back part of the callosum (the splenium) has been found to be larger in women. The anterior commissure is also larger in women. The massa intermedia is more often absent in men than in women.

Since that first report of a difference in callosal area between men and women, there have been both confirmations and denials. The consensus seems to be that there is probably a small difference in size favoring women. Some have claimed that this difference is restricted to the posterior region (called the *splenium*) (figure 10.2), and in several reports it appears only if a correction is made for the larger size of men's brains (see Driesen and Raz, 1995, for review). Whenever we compare the size of a structure in men and women, we must keep in mind that since men's brains are larger, any *particular* structure may be also be larger in men than in women.

There appears to be less controversy about the sex difference found in another smaller commissural system, the *anterior commissure*. Researchers in Gorski's lab have found that women have a larger cross-sectional area through the anterior commissure than men do, even when no correction is made for the smaller size of women's brains (Allen and Gorski, 1991). They also confirmed earlier reports that the massa intermedia, which connects the two sides of the thalamus, is more often absent in men than in women. When it is present, it is larger in women. Finally, they found that homosexual men had larger anterior commissures than heterosexual men, and that their commissures were at least as large as in heterosexual women, depending on whether or not measurements were corrected for brain size.

What is the significance of a larger commissural area? The simple interpretation would be that there are more nerve fibers in a larger commissure than in a smaller one, and therefore potentially more or better connections between the two hemispheres. That the greater callosal area does indicate a larger number of fibers crossing between the hemispheres is borne out in a study on human brains (Aboitiz, Scheibel, Fisher, and Zaidel, 1992). Thus cognitive functions that typically rely on one hemisphere might be more likely to be shared or made available to the other hemisphere; that is, such functions would be somewhat less strictly dependent on one hemisphere. This arrangement might make some difference to how one solves problems. For example, if presented with a nonverbal problem like some of those described in the chapter on spatial abilities (chapter 5), a person with better connections between the hemispheres might be more likely to employ words in finding a solution. While this is only a speculation at present, it is a reasonable one.

Whether a greater sharing of function between hemispheres is an advantage or not probably depends on the particular cognitive ability. Some skills might be improved by having ready communication between hemispheres, whereas for skills that need a very focal neural organization—possibly certain motor skills—this could be a disadvantage. We have no evidence yet that any cognitive skill is better (or worse) in women than in men, as a result of differing commissural pathways. However, one study restricted to women found a significant positive relation between the size of the splenial area of the corpus callosum and performance on verbal fluency tasks (Hines, Chiu, McAdams, Bentler and Lipcamon, 1992). Those women with larger splenia had better scores in tasks requiring them to generate words or sentences with constraints on their beginning letters (as described in chapter 8). Since no men were tested in that study, we don't know whether the higher verbal fluency often found in women could be accounted for by women's larger commissural areas.

It would seem to follow that better transmission of information between left and right halves of the brain should in some way alter the division of labour between the hemispheres. We have learned from studying people with damage to various parts of the brain that the left hemisphere is critical for speaking and most other language skills, whereas the right hemisphere plays a larger role in certain perceptual and spatial abilities. This division is often referred to as *lateralization* of function. Variation in numbers of commissural fibers might influence this hemispheric specialization in at least two ways. First, if commissural systems are enhanced from the start, or early in life, the trading of information between hemispheres might actually affect the *development* of hemispheric specialization of function. People with larger commissures might be less lateralized for speech, spatial ability, or other functions that depend more on one or the other hemisphere.

Alternatively, development of left and right hemispheric specialization might go on in more or less the same way regardless of the size of the commissural area; but while actually engaged in a cognitive task dependent on one hemisphere, people with larger commissures may approach it differently because information from the other hemisphere is more readily available. It has even been suggested that increased commissural connections might *enhance* hemispheric lateralization, because stronger connections between hemispheres might make it easier for one hemisphere to inhibit the activity of the other.

Hemispheric Asymmetry

Other ways of producing variation in brain asymmetry are related to the development of the hemispheres themselves. For example, the growth or number of neurons in each hemisphere might not be equal in males and females. We know that in male rodents, but not in females, the outer layer of the brain, the *cortex*, is thicker on the right than on the left (Diamond, Dowling, and Johnson, 1981). This asymmetry is apparently caused by androgens, since male rats castrated at birth—which stops the flow of androgens from the testes to the brain—show no such difference in cortical thickness. In the human male fetus a difference in volume favoring the right hemisphere has also been reported (deLacoste, Horvath, and Woodward, 1991), but so far no equivalent pattern has been reported in adults. If such a difference were present in adult men, it might be one means of enhancing functions, such as visuospatial abilities, that are especially dependent on the right hemisphere. Just such an explanation has been offered by Geschwind (Geschwind and Galaburda, 1985) who proposed that early testicular androgens have the same effect in humans as in rodents—enhancing the growth of the right hemisphere relative to the left. As we shall suggest in chapter 11, however, this explanation for men's spatial skills may not hold in humans.

Alterations in hemispheric asymmetry restricted to particular areas could also affect the way cognitive functions are organized. One region of the brain that is noticably different in area in the two hemispheres is the *planum temporale*, the area on the upper surface of the temporal lobe behind the primary auditory area (see figure 10.1). The planum temporale on the left side is known to be important for the perception of speech sounds, and in most people, this area is larger than the comparable area on the right (Geschwind and Levitsky, 1968). It has been claimed that the degree of leftward asymmetry is less in females as a group than in males, although this sex difference, if it exists, is very small. This finding, like claims for several other morphological sex differences, has been contested; and it appears that in the two main studies in which sample sizes were sufficiently large (Wada, Clarke and Hamm, 1975; Jäncke, Schlaug, Huang, and Steinmetz, 1994), the difference between the sexes is fairly trivial.

In contrast, a recent study of sex differences in hemispheric asymmetry has found what appear to be relatively large differences in another cortical region, the *planum parietale*. This area is a part of the parietal lobe at the posterior end of the Sylvian fissure (see figure 10.1). In the left hemisphere in right-handers, it contributes significantly to control of speech and manual movements, though perhaps only in men (see chapter 11). On the right side, it appears to contribute to spatial ability. A measure comparing the surface area of the planum parietale of left and right sides showed overall a rightward-larger asymmetry, which may relate to its important contribution in visuospatial processing. However, in right-handers the rightward bias appeared to be larger in men than in women (figure 10.3) (Jäncke et al., 1994).

The findings for left-handers was just the reverse—left-handed women showed a much larger rightward asymmetry of this parietal region than

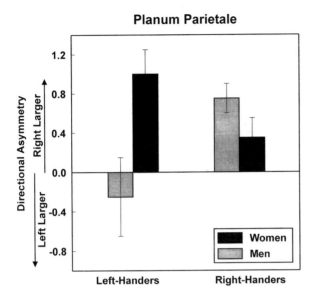

Figure 10.3
Directional asymmetry in the planum parietale. Overall, the planum parietale is larger on the right than the left. In right-handers, this rightward asymmetry is greater in men; whereas in left-handers the pattern is reversed. (Modified from Jäncke et al., 1994. (Reproduced by permission of the authors.)

left-handed men did; the latter actually showed a small leftward bias. No information on the cognitive patterns of these subjects was available, but other data suggest that handedness may interact with sex (and with intelligence level) to influence spatial ability. In some comparisons, left-handed women have better spatial scores than left-handed men (Harshman, Hampson, and Berenbaum, 1983), a pattern different from that of right-handers. So we may speculate that variation in the size of the planum parietale, or in its degree of rightward asymmetry, predicts spatial ability of some kind.

Variations in hemispheric functional asymmetry may arise in the absence of gross visible structural variations. There could well be variation in asymmetry at a more cellular level (e.g., in the size, or number of branches, of parts of the neurons; or in distribution of neurotransmitters) that could mediate cognitive differences. Variations in fiber connections between neurocognitive systems, such as within hemispheres, could also result in different cognitive patterns. It is hard, in fact, to imagine any variation in brain morphology or molecular substructure that would not have some effect on problem-solving behaviors at some point. The other side of the coin is that findings of individual differences in *functional* brain asymmetry must reflect some parallel physiological differences, even if they are not visible to the naked eye.

Some of the evidence in favor of sex differences in brain asymmetry comes from special research techniques used in normal people, comparing the left and right ears, visual fields, or hands. This kind of study is made possible by the fact that one side of the brain tends to control basic motor and sensory function primarily on the opposite side of the body. For example, although both ears have connections with the specialized cortical area in each hemisphere which receives auditory input, the crossed pathways (from ear to opposite hemisphere) are stronger than the uncrossed. This means that the right ear has better connections with the left hemisphere than does the left ear, which in turn has better connections with the right hemisphere. When different words are presented to the two ears at the same time (in what is called *dichotic* presentation), the listener doesn't report all words correctly. The words presented to the right ear are usually reported more accurately because they have better access to the left hemisphere, where the sounds are analyzed as speech (Kimura, 1961). Melodic patterns, however, which are processed better by the right hemisphere, are perceived more accurately when they arrive at the left ear (Kimura, 1964). This is not due to any difference between the ears themselves, but to their different points of arrival in the brain (figure 10.4).

In the visual system, the arrangement is somewhat different. In humans, each eye has roughly equal connections with each hemisphere, so we can't simply compare what happens when a stimulus is presented to the left or the right eye.[1] Instead, each visual *field*, that is the visual array you see to the left or the right of your nose when you look straight ahead, is represented in the opposite hemisphere (figure 10.5). So the left visual field sends light images to the right half of each retina, which relays information to the right hemisphere. Since under normal viewing conditions we can't show things to only one visual field—because people naturally shift their gaze to wherever the stimulus is—we use a device called a tachistoscope. This apparatus flashes a stimulus so briefly that

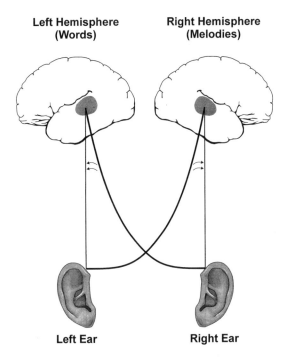

Left Hemisphere
(Words)

Right Hemisphere
(Melodies)

Left Ear

Right Ear

Figure 10.4
Depiction of dichotic listening. Because the crossed pathways are stronger, when two different sounds are presented to the two ears simultaneously, words coming to the right ear have the advantage in better access to the left hemisphere; whereas melodic patterns from the left ear are advantaged.

the eyes cannot fixate on a new location during the presentation. So researchers ask the subject to stare at a central point, while they present an image quickly in either the left or right visual field (figure 10.5).

The resulting pattern is similar to what happens in dichotic listening. Words and letters, which depend more on the left hemisphere for perception, are reported more accurately in the right visual field; whereas the accurate location of a dot in space, which depends more on the right hemisphere, is better in the left visual field (Kimura, 1966).

Both men and women show these perceptual asymmetries, but some studies report that the difference between ears or visual fields is larger in men than in women (e.g., Lake and Bryden, 1976; Weekes, Zaidel, and Zaidel, 1995). This might mean that the functions of the two hemispheres

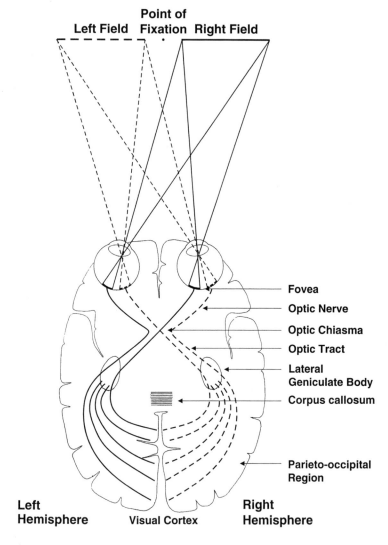

Figure 10.5
Left and right visual fields and their pathways to the visual cortex of the two hemispheres. To present a stimulus exclusively to one hemisphere, it must be flashed in one visual field very briefly, while the subject is fixating on a central point. This is what a tachistoscope does.

are not as sharply differentiated in women. Alternatively it may indicate that, because of the better connections between hemispheres in women, discussed above, information from one ear or visual field is transmitted more accurately from the opposite hemisphere to the hemisphere on the *same* side. For example, words coming to the left ear would stimulate primarily the right hemisphere but because of additional commissural connections in women, might also be more accurately transmitted from the right hemisphere to the left. This mechanism could reduce the difference between scores for the two ears, even if the hemispheres are as asymmetric as in men. Other ways in which men's and women's brain organizations differ, and which could yield smaller ear or visual field differences in women are discussed in chapter 11.

Note

1. Unfortunately, at least one of the critics of the idea that sex differences in cognition might be related to differences in brain organization has misunderstood this arrangement in the visual system. (Fausto-Sterling A. *Myths of gender*. New York: Basic Books, 1992, 2nd edition, p. 52.)

Further Reading

Aboitiz F., Scheibel A.B., Fisher R.S. & Zaidel E. (1992) Fiber composition of the human corpus callosum. *Brain Research*, *598*, 143–153.

Allen L.S. & Gorski R.A. (1991) Sexual dimorphism of the anterior commissure and massa intermedia of the human brain. *Journal of Comparative Neurology*, *312*, 97–104.

Allen L.S. & Gorski R.A. (1992) Sexual orientation and the size of the anterior commissure in the human brain. *Proceedings of the National Academy of Sciences*, *89*, 7199–7202.

Allen L.S., Hines M., Shryne J.E. & Gorski R.A. (1989) Two sexually dimorphic cell groups in the human brain. *Journal of Neuroscience*, *9*, 497–506.

Alexopoulos D.S. (1996) Sex differences and IQ. *Personality & Individual Differences*, *20*, 445–450.

Andreasen N.C., Swayze V., O'Leary D.S., Alliger R., Cohen G., Ehrhardt J. & Yuh W.T.C. (1993) Intelligence and brain structure in normal individuals. *American Journal of Psychiatry*, *150*, 130–134.

Ankney C.D. (1992) Sex differences in relative brain size: the mismeasure of woman, too? *Intelligence*, *16*, 329–336.

deLacoste-Utamsing M.C. & Holloway R.L. (1982) Sexual dimorphism in the human corpus callosum. *Science, 216*, 1431–1432.

deLacoste M.C., Horvath D.S. & Woodward D.J. (1991) Possible sex differences in the developing human fetal brain. *Journal of Clinical and Experimental Neuropsychology, 13*, 831–846.

Diamond M.C., Dowling G.A. & Johnson R.E. (1981) Morphological cerebral cortical asymmetry in male and female rats. *Experimental Neurology, 71*, 261–268.

Driesen N.R. & Raz N. (1995) The influence of sex, age, and handedness on corpus callosum morphology. A meta-analysis. *Psychobiology, 23*, 240–247.

Geschwind N. & Galaburda A.M. (1985) Cerebral lateralization. Biological mechanisms, associations, and pathology: I. A hypothesis and a program for research. *Archives of Neurology, 42*, 428–459.

Geschwind N. & Levitsky W. (1968) Human brain: left-right asymmetries in temporal speech region. *Science, 161*, 186–187.

Hall J.A. & Kimura D. (1993) Homosexuality and circadian rhythms. *Neuropsychopharmacology Supplement Abstracts, 9*, 1265.

Harshman R.A., Hampson E. & Berenbaum S.A. (1983) Individual differences in cognitive abiities and brain organization, Part I: Sex and handedness differences in ability. *Canadian Journal of Psychology, 37*, 144–192.

Hines M., Chiu L., McAdams L.A., Bentler P.M. & Lipcamon J. (1992) Cognition and the corpus callosum: verbal fluency, visuospatial ability and language lateralization related to midsagittal surface areas of callosal subregions. *Behavioral Neuroscience, 106*, 3–14.

Jacobson C.D., Csernus V.J., Shryne J.E. & Gorski R.A. (1981) The influence of gonadectomy, androgen exposure, or a gonadal graft in the neonatal rat on the volume of the sexually dimorphic nucleus of the preoptic area. *Journal of Neuroscience, 1*, 1142–1147.

Jäncke L., Schlaug G., Huang Y. & Steinmetz H. (1994) Asymmetry of the planum parietale. *NeuroReport, 5*, 1161–1163.

Kimura, D. (1961) Cerebral dominance and the perception of verbal stimuli. *Canadian Journal of Psychology, 15*, 166–171.

Kimura D. (1966) Dual functional asymmetry of the brain in visual perception. *Neuropsychologia, 4*, 275–285.

Kimura D. (1964) Left-right differences in the perception of melodies. *Quarterly Journal of Experimental Psychology, 16*, 355–358.

Lake D.A. & Bryden M.P. (1976) Handedness and sex differences in hemispheric asymmetry. *Brain & Language, 3*, 266–282.

LeVay S. (1991) A difference in hypothalamic structure between heterosexual and homosexual men. *Science, 253*, 1034–1037.

Lucas T.H., Lombardino L.J., Roper S.N. & Leonard C.M. (1996) Effects of handedness and gender on hippocampal size in normal children: an MRI study. *Society for Neuroscience Abstracts*, 22, 1860 (Abstract 730.12).

Lynn R. (1994) Sex differences in intelligence and brain size: a paradox resolved. *Personality & Individual Differences*, 17, 257–271.

Lynn R. (1998) Sex differences in intelligence: A rejoinder to Mackintosh. *Journal of Biosocial Science*, 30, 529–532.

Mackintosh N.J. (1998) Reply to Lynn. *Journal of Biosocial Science*, 30, 533–539.

Maxson S.C. (1997) Sex differences in genetic mechanisms for mammalian brain and behavior. *Biomedical Reviews*, 7, 85–90.

Milner B. (1968) Further analysis of the hippocampal amnesic syndrome: 14-year follow-up study of H.M. *Neuropsychologia*, 6, 215–234.

Olton D.S. (1977) Spatial memory. *Scientific American*, 236, 82–98.

Pakkenberg B. & Gundersen H.J.G. (1997) Neocortical neuron number in humans: effect of sex and age. *Journal of Comparative Neurology*, 384, 312–320.

Roof R.L. & Havens M.D. (1992) Testosterone improves maze performance and induces development of a male hippocampus in females. *Brain Research*, 572, 310–313.

Sherry D.F., Jacobs L.F. & Gaulin S.J.C. (1992) Spatial memory and adaptive specialization of the hippocampus. *Trends in Neurosciences*, 15, 298–303.

Sherry D.F., Vaccarino A.L., Buckenham K. & Herz R.S. (1989) The hippocampal complex of food-storing birds. *Brain, Behavior and Evolution*, 34, 308–317.

Swaab D.F. & Hofman M.A. (1995) Sexual differentiation of the human hypothalamus in relation to gender and sexual orientation. *Trends in Neurosciences*, 18, 264–270.

Wada J.A., Clarke R. & Hamm A. (1975) Cerebral hemispheric asymmetry in humans. *Archives of Neurology*, 32, 239–246.

Weekes N.Y., Zaidel D.W. & Zaidel E. (1995) Effects of sex and sex role attributions on the ear advantage in dichotic listening. *Neuropsychology*, 9, 62–67.

Wickett J.C., Vernon P.A. & Lee D.H. (1996) General intelligence and brain volume in a sample of healthy adult male siblings. *International Journal of Psychology*, 31, 238–239.

Wickett J.C., Vernon P.A., & Lee D.H. (1994) *In vivo* brain size, head perimeter, and intelligence in a sample of healthy adult females. *Personality & Individual Differences*, 16, 831–838.

Willerman L., Rutledge J.N. & Bigler E.D. (1991) *In vivo* brain size and intelligence. *Intelligence*, 15, 223–228.

Zhou J.N., Hofman M.A., Gooren L.J.G. & Swaab D.F. (1995) A sex difference in the human brain and its relation to transsexuality. *Nature*, 378, 68–70.

11

Brain Mechanisms Studied in Damaged Brains

In the preceding chapter we discussed evidence that the degree of cerebral lateralization, or functional asymmetry, of the brain might not be as great in women as in men. Further evidence that the left and right hemispheres may not be as differentiated in women comes from studying the effects of injury to one hemisphere of the brain. This kind of restricted damage most often results from strokes (in which the arteries supplying blood to one hemisphere are obstructed) or from the growth of tumors, although pathology may also result from other sources. By studying people who have malfunction of limited areas of the brain, we can learn a great deal about how those areas contribute to human cognitive function. Fortunately, most patients are willing to volunteer for such research (even though they themselves may not benefit directly from it), in the hope of helping other future patients or advancing the cause of science. Without their cooperation, we would know much less than we do about human brain function.

A severe speech disorder called *aphasia* is less likely to happen to women than men after left-hemisphere damage. Aphasia is typically defined as the inability to accurately perform such simple verbal tasks as counting, saying the days of the week, naming objects, or following simple instructions. The fact that in women such aphasic disorders are less common after left-hemisphere pathology has been taken to mean that their speech is more bilaterally organized than men's, that it is more equally shared by the two hemispheres. If speech functions involve both hemispheres, we would expect damage to one hemisphere to be less likely to cause a speech disturbance.

Another line of evidence for the idea that women have a more bilateral speech organization than men is the occasional claim that women who do suffer from aphasia recover better or more quickly than aphasic men do (Basso, Capitani, and Moraschini, 1982; Pizzamiglia and Mammucari, 1985). This fact again might suggest that, in women, speech is more diffusely represented. If, for example, the right hemisphere were more involved with speech functions in women than in men, it could presumably take over some of the functions affected by the left-hemisphere damage, and allow speech to recover more quickly or more completely.

One problem with that schema is that there is no evidence that aphasia occurs more often after right-hemisphere damage in women than in men. Yet this should happen if in women speech is more dependent on the right side of the brain than is the case for men. In fact, however, in our own series of patients with adult damage, aphasia after right-hemisphere pathology was extremely rare, and was certainly not more common in women. As we shall suggest below, the lower incidence of aphasia after left-hemisphere pathology in women might instead be due to a different organization *within* the left hemisphere.

Although there is no evidence that basic speech functions, as manifest in outright aphasia, are any more dependent on the right hemisphere in women than in men, other less basic verbal functions might be. Studying higher-level verbal functioning in patients who were not aphasic suggested that some of these functions might be more bilaterally organized in women. For example, in our series of nonaphasic patients, scores on a vocabulary test, in which words had to be defined, were affected by both left- and right-hemisphere damage in women. In men, vocabulary scores were affected only by left-hemisphere damage (Kimura and Harshman, 1984). This suggests that some abstract or complex verbal skills may be more bilaterally organized in women than in men. However, women do not have better vocabulary scores than men do, which raises questions about the idea that bilateral organization of verbal functions in women enhances their verbal skills (Springer and Deutsch, 1981).

However, we may still ask whether those verbal skills at which women *do* excel are more bilaterally organized in women than in men. We have some information bearing on this question for two such abilities—verbal fluency and verbal memory.

Verbal Fluency

By verbal fluency in this instance we mean specifically the ability to say as many words as possible beginning with a particular letter within a specified time period. As one might expect, this ability is generally affected more by damage to the left hemisphere than to the right, even in nonaphasic patients. The region especially critical for such verbal fluency is the anterior part of the hemisphere, that area in front of the central fissure (figure 10.1) (Milner, 1964). We therefore calculated the average scores for men and women who had had damage to this region in either hemisphere.

As figure 11.1 shows, the lowest scores were those of men with left-hemisphere damage; they were much lower than the scores of men with right-hemisphere damage. However, the scores of the two female groups did not differ. Recall from chapter 8 that normal women (those

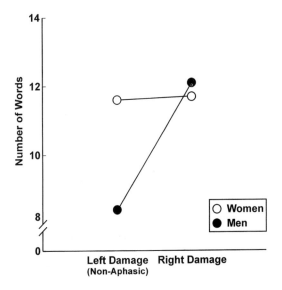

Figure 11.1
Verbal Fluency after left- or right-hemisphere pathology. The patient says as many words as possible beginning with a designated letter. Women generally get higher scores on this test, and it appears that this skill is more bilaterally organized in women than in men, since it is equally affected by left- or right-hemisphere damage.

with no brain damage) get better scores than normal men. Women patients with posterior damage (outside these critical anterior regions) also got higher scores than comparable men. So it appears that women's verbal fluency scores are slightly affected by anterior damage to either the left or the right hemisphere; that is, that like vocabulary, ability in fluency is more bilaterally organized in women than in men. This finding agrees with a report arising from the injection of sodium amytal into each hemisphere in turn, to determine in which hemisphere speech is represented. The effect of the injection lasts for a few minutes only, but while one hemisphere is incapacitated, we can test for various abilities to investigate the functions of that hemisphere. Women showed a drop in fluency after injection of either hemisphere, whereas men showed a decline only after a left-hemisphere injection (McGlone and Fox, 1982).

Of course one is tempted to think that the more bilateral organization of verbal fluency in women is the basis for their advantage on that function. But will this necessarily be true for other verbal functions at which women excel? Let's look at another such function, verbal memory.

Verbal Memory

The measure employed in this research was the combined recall score, after about an hour, for two stories read aloud to the patients, plus the number of words remembered from a list of spoken word pairs. Verbal memory is known to be affected by damage to the left temporal region (Milner, 1967), and it is more likely to be affected after a delay than when tested immediately after the presentation of the material.

For these tasks, there was a clear effect of left-hemisphere damage in both men and women (figure 11.2), in that the scores for patients with left temporal pathology were worse than those of patients with right temporal pathology. There was no suggestion of a more bilateral organization in women; that is, left temporal damage affected scores to the same degree in both sexes, though again, women had better scores overall. So here we have a quite different pattern, an ability that is clearly better in women than in men, but that is apparently lateralized to the left hemisphere to the same degree in the two sexes.

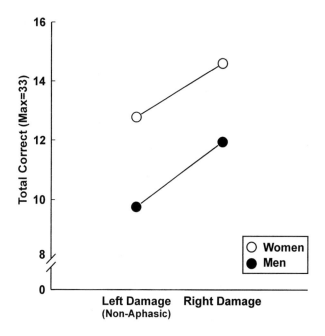

Figure 11.2
Verbal Memory: the recall, after a delay, of short stories and word pairs. Women also get higher scores on this kind of test, but verbal memory does not appear to be more bilaterally organized in women. Both men and women are more affected by left-hemisphere damage.

It seems apparent from such studies that we cannot make any general statement about whether having a more or less bilateral brain organization for a verbal function will be of any advantage for that function. What about the visuospatial functions (some of which were described in chapter 5) which depend more on the right hemisphere? Is there any evidence from neurological patients that such functions are more right-hemisphere dependent in men than in women? We report below on two studies which bear on this question.

Spatial Blocks

In our lab, we administered a task employing spatial blocks to a series of patients with damage restricted to either the left or right hemisphere. The method used required no spoken response, so that aphasic patients could be tested. The test employed two actual 3-dimensional blocks that were mirror images of each other (figure 11.3). The patients were shown a series of photographs of these blocks in various orientations, and were required to place each photograph in front of the block depicted in the photo. To do so, they had to imagine what the blocks would look like when turned in various ways, so this was a test of imaginal rotation.

As expected, patients with right-hemisphere damage had lower scores than those with left-hemisphere damage (figure 11.4); and women overall had lower scores than men did. However, a right- hemisphere lesion had no greater effect on men than on women, which should have been the case if spatial rotation were more asymmetrically organized in men, that is, more dependent on the right hemisphere.

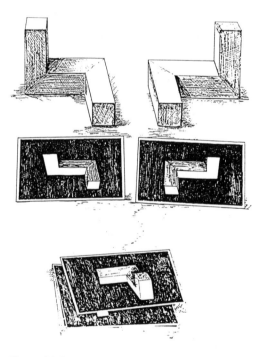

Figure 11.3
A Spatial Rotation task. The patient must decide which of the two blocks are depicted in each of a series of photographs, and place each photo in front of the correct block.

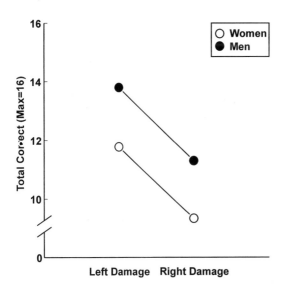

Figure 11.4
Scores on the spatial task shown in figure 11.3 after left- or right-hemisphere pathology. Although men score higher than women overall, and right-hemisphere damage lowers scores relative to left-hemisphere damage, there seems to be no difference between men and women in the degree to which this ability depends on the right hemisphere.

Line Orientation

A study from another lab (Desmond, Glenwick, Stern, and Tatemichi, 1994) used a quite different spatial task. Two lines at different angles to the horizontal were presented, and had to be identified on a card showing 12 different line angles (figure 11.5) (Benton, Hamsher, Varney, and Spreen, 1983). Earlier research with this type of task had found that men get better scores overall, and that damage to the right hemisphere affects this ability. In the Desmond study, both of these things held true. However, although men's performance on this task was affected by right-hemisphere strokes, women were, if anything, more affected (figure 11.6). That is, the difference between normal women and those with right-hemisphere damage appeared even larger than the difference between corresponding groups of men.

What information we have, then, does not support the idea that general-

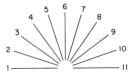

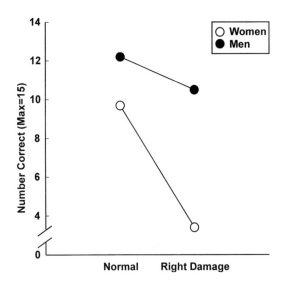

Figure 11.5
Example from the Benton Line Orientation task. The subject has to match the slopes of the two lines shown at top with specific lines in the larger array at bottom. (From Benton et al., 1983. Copyright 1983, 1994 Oxford University Press. Used by permission of Oxford University Press.)

Figure 11.6
Ability to identify the slope of a line after right-hemisphere damage. If anything, it appears that *women* are more affected than men by injury to the right hemisphere. (After Desmond et al., 1994.)

Table 11.1
Lateralization and sex advantage

Primarily Left Unilateral in Both Sexes	
Verbal Memory	F>
Presumptively More Bilateral in Women	
Verbal Fluency	F>
Vocabulary	N
Primarily Right Unilateral in Both Sexes	
Mental Rotation	M>
Line Orientation	M>
Stereoscopic Fusion	F>
Identifying Facial Expression	F>

F>= female advantage, M>= male advantage, N>= no sex difference

ized damage to the right hemisphere has any greater effect on spatial ability in men than in women. The differences between normal men and women that we routinely see on spatial tasks do not seem to be mediated by obvious differences in hemispheric functional asymmetry (table 11.1). There must be some other basis for the sex difference in spatial rotation.

It doesn't seem to be true, either, that men are better on all tasks that depend more on the right than the left hemisphere, which is what one might expect from Geschwind's suggestion that androgens enhance right-hemisphere functioning in men. We know from several studies, for example, that the fusion of the images from the two eyes which gives us information about depth (see Chapter 7) is more dependent on the right hemisphere. Yet this ability appears to be greater in women than in men. The same could be said for the processing of facial expression—it appears to be better in women yet it too is more right-hemisphere dependent (Levy and Heller, 1992).

Intrahemispheric Organization

Besides the possible differences between the sexes in commissural connections and in hemispheric specialization, there appears to be a difference in the organization of functions *within* a hemisphere. This was first discovered for the representation of speech and certain motor control functions within the left hemisphere, but it may also hold for some aspects of right-hemisphere functioning.

The left hemisphere is critical not only for speech and other communicative systems such as manual sign language, but also for certain complex motor functions unrelated to language. Though we will not discuss the idea at length here, it has in fact been proposed that the specialization of the left hemisphere for communicative function arose out of its critical role in the control of oral and manual movements (Kimura, 1993). Patients with left-hemisphere damage, in addition to their trouble in communicating, often have difficulty in performing some noncommunicative manual and oral movements. For example, they make errors in showing how to use certain objects such as scissors or a hammer, or in making intransitive movements (those not directed at objects) such as saluting or waving goodbye. That the movements in which problems appear need not be symbolic or representative of anything else is shown by the fact that such patients also make errors in copying a series of totally meaningless unfamiliar hand and arm movements (figure 11.7). They are said to have *apraxia*, or be *manually apraxic*. Some patients have similar problems with imitation of nonspeech oral movements (e.g., sticking out the tongue, pursing the lips), a condition described as *oral apraxia*.

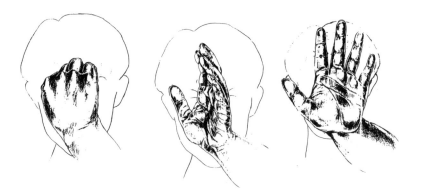

Figure 11.7
Example of one item used to assess manual apraxia. The researcher makes the movements and the patient simply copies them.

We were interested in comparing the contributions of different regions of the left hemisphere to such motor and speech functions. Initially, therefore, we had to remove from consideration those patients who had widespread damage to the left hemisphere, which is generally over half of stroke patients. We then considered patients whose damage was restricted to the posterior part of the brain (including the temporal lobe) separately from those with damage to the anterior or front part of the brain. We tallied the number of patients who were aphasic, as determined by a standard test for aphasia, in each group. It soon became clear that men and women differed markedly in this respect (figure 11.8).

Women were more likely to be aphasic if the damage was to the anterior region, whereas men showed the reverse pattern (Kimura, 1983, 1993). When we looked at subdivisions within the posterior region,

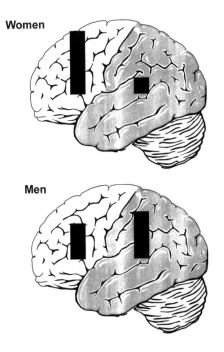

Figure 11.8
Incidence of speech disorders (aphasias) after left anterior or posterior damage. In women, the incidence of aphasia is higher after anterior damage. The reverse is true in men.

aphasia was equally likely to occur in men and women if the temporal lobe was affected. However, if it was the parietal lobe that was damaged, men were much more likely to become aphasic, so the difference between the sexes was most obvious in the parietal region. Remember that we did not find a higher incidence of aphasia in women after right-hemisphere damage. This suggests that whatever speech functions the parietal lobe serves in men must be served in women by other areas of the left hemisphere. It seems likely that for women some part of the anterior area in the left hemisphere is responsible for such functions.

Plotting the incidence of manual apraxia, as measured by the score in copying unfamiliar movements like those depicted in figure 11.7, reveals an even sharper difference between men and women. There are very few apraxic women after posterior damage and very few apraxic men after anterior damage (figure 11.9). One basis for the sharper differentiation in

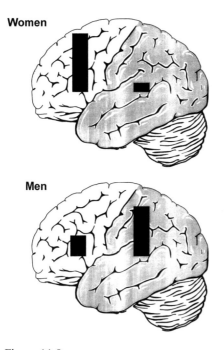

Figure 11.9
Incidence of manual apraxia after left anterior or posterior damage. The patterns for men and women are similar to those for aphasia (figure 11.8).

apraxia is that damage to the temporal lobe, which may result in speech problems in both sexes, does not typically make patients apraxic. So we are really seeing the difference between damage to primarily parietal and primarily frontal areas.

This difference between men and women in the intrahemispheric control centers for certain actions may be seen also in the right hemisphere. For example, on one task, Block Design, which requires using the hands to assemble blocks to make a designated spatial pattern (see figure 9.3), there is a similar effect. Block Design scores are impaired by both left- and right-hemisphere pathology in both sexes, probably because it requires both motor planning and spatial analysis. However, as figure 11.10 shows, women's scores are more affected by right anterior damage, and men's by right posterior damage.

Why should there be such a difference between the sexes in brain organization? Does it relate to the way they perform certain actions? The answer to the latter question is almost certainly yes, but at present we have no clues to exactly how it matters whether complex motor control is more dependent on anterior or posterior areas. The reader will recall from chapter 4 that men and women do differ in the kind of motor skills at which they excel,

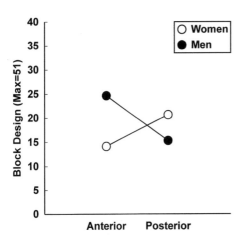

Figure 11.10
Scores on a constructional task (Block Design) after right anterior or posterior damage. Women's scores are more affected by right anterior damage and men's by posterior damage.

with women tending to be better at fine motor or small-amplitude skills involving fingers and hands. In contrast men are better at large-amplitude skills like targeting—throwing missiles to points outside personal space. We may speculate that for accurate extrapersonal aiming, it is important to mesh the motor aspects of the task, the throwing movements, with visual information about the location of the target. It may therefore be advantageous to have motor organizing systems closer to the visual area, which is at the back of the brain. In women, fine motor skills might be enhanced by having such an organizing system in close proximity to the motor cortex (in the front part of the brain), which is critical for finger control. Only further research can answer these questions.

A secondary result of finding a sex difference in intrahemispheric organization is that it may shed light on the sex difference in the frequency of aphasia after left-hemisphere damage, mentioned earlier in this chapter. Women become aphasic less often than men with this condition. This may be due to the fact that damage to the posterior part of the hemisphere is more common after strokes than damage to the anterior part. If men's speech is more dependent on the left posterior area, it would be affected by a stroke more often than a woman's more anterior speech area would be. These findings suggest that, so far from women's basic speech functions being more diffusely organized in the brain, they are at least as focally represented as men's, albeit differently organized.

Such findings from damage to the brain also have some implications for interpreting the sex differences sometimes seen in studies of perceptual asymmetry. Recall, for example, that right-ear superiority for dichotically presented words is sometimes reported to be greater in men than in women. This has often been taken to mean that women's brains are less asymmetrically organized for speech than men's. But an alternative interpretation might be that the left-hemisphere centers for processing speech sounds are located somewhat differently in women than in men, with the critical systems engaging the frontal brain areas more in women. Words arriving at the cortical auditory areas in the superior part of the temporal lobe have readier neural connections to the regions just posterior to this (critical for speech in men) than to the frontal speech areas (critical in women) (see figure 10.1). This could mean that it is easier to detect the left hemisphere's role in speech processing in men using dichotic listening, but it need not mean that their hemispheres are more asymmetric. The sex differences in perceptual asymmetry may simply be due to a limitation of the dichotic (and tachistoscopic) techniques.

Until very recently, relating brain characteristics to cognitive function relied primarily on information gained from postmortem data, from the cognitive deficits in patients with known lesions, or from the perceptual asymmetries detectible in normal persons. However, in the last few years it has become possible to get a picture of a person's brain by various new brain-imaging techniques. These include positron emission tomography (PET scan) and, more recently, functional magnetic resonance imaging (fMRI). This means that a normal person (without brain damage) can now have his or her brain "scanned" while working on a variety of cognitive tasks, to discover which brain areas are most active during such tasks. If there are differences in the way people perform the task, in terms of which neural systems they engage, this should eventually become apparent. These new imaging techniques will undoubtedly add enormously to our information about brain organization, including information about sex differences in such organization.

However, at this stage of our knowledge, we need to be cautious about what such techniques tell us. Currently, wide areas of the brain "light up" on an fMRI scan when a person is performing even a simple task. This is to be expected, since we can assume that many neural systems may come into play with any cognitive activity. It will be some time before we know which of the active areas are essential to the performance of a task and which are secondary. Most current imaging methods also require several trials on a task before the regions affected by it can be identified. For these reasons, information about what happens when a brain area is lost or removed, as occurs with actual damage to the brain, is still the best indicator of the critical systems for a given function. So we will need to study the effects of brain lesions, along with imaging data, to give us complete answers.

Summary

Although we know a great deal about how men and women differ in cognitive function, and quite a lot about how their brains differ, these two bodies of information have not yet coalesced. Women appear to have larger areas of connective fibers between the two hemispheres, making it probable that communication between their hemispheres is facilitated. It has also been suggested that the difference in function between the left and right hemispheres is more marked in men. One source of information about this hemispheric asymmetry is the left-right differences we detect by means of perceptual techniques that sample the functions of the opposite hemisphere. These include dichotic listening (presentation of different auditory stimuli to left and right ears) and tachistoscopic methods (presentation of visual stimuli very briefly to left and right visual fields). Such perceptual asymmetries are sometimes larger in men than in women. As well, speech disorders are more common after left-hemisphere damage in men than in women, and these findings have led some researchers to conclude that speech is more asymmetrically organized in men.

However, other evidence that speech and related motor functions are differently organized *within* the left hemisphere in men and women suggests alternative explanations. Aphasia and apraxia, which are more likely to occur after left anterior damage in women, occur more frequently in men after posterior damage. This finding suggests that men's and women's speech and praxic functions are more dependent, respectively, on posterior and anterior areas. Such variation in brain organization for speech may also affect the overall incidence of aphasia after left-hemisphere damage and the likelihood that right-ear or right-field perceptual advantages will appear in normal men and women.

Finally, there seems to be no simple or systematic relation between whether a particular function is more unilaterally or bilaterally organized, and whether it is better in men or women.

Further Reading

Basso A., Capitani E. & Moraschini S. (1982) Sex differences in recovery from aphasia. *Cortex*, *18*, 469–475.

Benton A.L., Hamsher K.D., Varney N.R. & Spreen O. (1983) *Contributions to neuropsychological assessment: a clinical manual*. New York: Oxford.

Desmond D.W., Glenwick D.S., Stern Y. & Tatemichi T.K. (1994) Sex differences in the representation of visuospatial function in the human brain. *Rehabilitation Psychology*, *39*, 3–14.

Geschwind N. & Galaburda A.M. (1985) Cerebral lateralization. Biological mechanisms, associations, and pathology. I. A hypothesis and a program for research. *Archives of Neurology, 42,* 428–459.

Kimura D. (1977) Acquisition of a motor skill after left- hemisphere damage. *Brain, 100,* 527–542.

Kimura D. (1983) Sex differences in cerebral organization for speech and praxic functions. *Canadian Journal of Psychology, 37,* 19–35.

Kimura D. (1993) *Neuromotor mechanisms in human communication.* New York: Oxford University Press, chapter 10.

Kimura D. & Harshman R.A. (1984) Sex differences in brain organization for verbal and non-verbal functions. In G.J. DeVries, J.P.C. DeBruin, H.B.M. Uylings & M.A. Corner (Eds.), *Sex differences in the brain. Progress in brain research.* Amsterdam: Elsevier, pp. 423–439.

Levy J. & Heller W. (1992) Gender differences in human neuropsychological function. In A.A. Gerall, H. Moltz & I.L. Ward (Eds.), *Sexual differentiation,* Volume 11 of *Handbook of behavioral neurobiology.* New York: Plenum Press, pp. 245–274.

McGlone J. & Fox A.J. (1982) Evidence from sodium amytal studies of greater asymmetry of verbal representation in men compared to women. In H. Akimoto, H. Kazamatsuri, M. Seino & A. Ward (Eds.), *Advances in epileptology: XIIIth Epilepsy International Symposium.* New York: Raven press, pp. 389–391.

Milner B. (1964) Some effects of frontal lobectomy in man. In J.M. Warren & K. Akert (Eds.), *The frontal granular cortex and behavior.* New York: McGraw-Hill, pp. 313–331.

Milner B. (1967) Brain mechanisms suggested by studies of temporal lobes. In C.H. Millikan & F.L. Darley (Eds.), *Brain mechanisms underlying speech and language.* New York: Grune & Stratton, pp. 122–145.

Pizzamiglio L. & Mammucari A. (1985) Evidence for sex differences in brain organization in recovery in aphasia. *Brain & Language, 25,* 213–223.

Springer S.P. & Deutsch G. (1981) *Left brain, right brain.* San Francisco: W.H. Freeman & Co.

12

Body Asymmetry and Cognitive Pattern

Some researchers have theorized that androgens enhance the development of the right hemisphere of the brain (Geschwind and Galaburda, 1985). Some have even suggested that this is part of a generalized enhancement of the development of the right side of the body (Levy and Levy, 1978). The latter reported, as would be predicted from the androgenic theory, that the right foot was larger in men, and the left foot larger in women. Although others' attempts to repeat these findings have met with mixed success, the idea remains an intriguing one.

In mammals the gonads also appear to differ in size, with the right gonad typically larger. This difference has been confirmed in the human fetus for both the male (testes) and female (ovaries) gonads (Mittwoch and Mahadevaiah, 1980). In adult males also the right testis is, on average, larger than the left testis, but no comparable information on gonad asymmetry is available for adult women. Before the advent of ultrasound it would have been difficult to determine the size of the ovary in living women.

However, Mittwoch and Mahadevaiah also reported that human hermaphrodites, who have both male and female gonads, more often have ovaries on the left side, and testes on the right. This suggests that there may be some *functional* favoring of the left ovary and the right testis in ordinary men and women.

We know that the gonads secrete sex hormones directly into the bloodstream, which presumably affect both sides of the body equally. Curiously, however, there is also some evidence that each gonad exerts a direct neural influence on the hypothalamus of the brain on the *ipsilateral* (same) side, possibly via the vagus nerve (Gerendai, 1987). This could mean that the left gonad has a greater influence over the left hypothalamus, and the right gonad over the right hypothalamus. The hypothalamus in turn appears to have primarily ipsilateral control over the autonomic nervous system, which directs the functioning of the mammary glands. This arrangement would potentially allow any difference in the activity of the two ovaries to show itself in asymmetry of the mammary glands.

We first investigated the possible relation between body asymmetry and brain function by asking undergraduate volunteers to inspect their own testicular or breast asymmmetry and report to us. To our surprise, we found that men and women reported opposite prevailing asymmetries, paralleling Jerre Levy's findings on feet; that is, more men reported having a larger right testicle, but more women reported having a larger left breast. Published studies on both living men and cadavers have also shown a prevalence of a larger right testis (Chang, Hsu, Chan and Chan, 1960; Mittwoch, 1988), so it appears that our subjects reported their asymmetries fairly accurately.

The same students also completed a variety of cognitive tasks. They consisted of so-called masculine, feminine and neutral tests, that is, tests on which either males or females do better, or which typically show no difference between the sexes (see table 12.1). We found the typical sex differences, with men better at five of the six masculine tests, and women better at all three of the feminine tests (Kimura, 1994).

When we compared the cognitive patterns of people who reported that they had larger left testes or breasts with those reporting larger right testes or breasts, we found an unexpected difference. The left-larger group as a whole performed better on the female-favoring tasks than did the right-larger group. This was true of *both* men and women, so it was not due to the fact that there were more women in the left-larger group. The right-larger group, however, performed better than the left-larger group on the male-favoring tasks, and again this was true in both men and women. So when we subtracted each person's averaged feminine score from his or her masculine score, we saw a pattern in which the left-larger group and right-larger groups differed (figure 12.1). The neutral tasks showed no difference between the two groups.

When any two groups differ in cognitive functioning, we can assume that their brains are in some way different. So not only must male and

Table 12.1
Tests used in the body asymmetry study

Neutral Tests	
Vocabulary	
Raven's Matrices	(a visual reasoning task)
Inferences	(a verbal reasoning task)
"Feminine" Tests	
Finding a's	(a perceptual speed test; see chapter 7)
Identical Pictures	(a perceptual speed test; see chapter 7)
Things White, Red	(an "ideational" fluency task; see chapter 8)
"Masculine" Tests	
Math Aptitude	(Chapter 6)
Mental Rotation	(Chapter 5)
Paper Folding	(Chapter 5)
Benton Lines	(Chapters 5 and 11)
Hidden Figures	(Chapter 5)
Throwing Accuracy	(Chapter 4)

female brains be different in some way, but within each sex as well, the left-larger and right-larger groups must have somewhat different brain organizations. If the evidence in rodents for a direct neural influence from gonad to ipsilateral hypothalamus is found in people as well, it might suggest that the left and right hypothalamus do not function identically in women and men, nor in leftward and rightward body asymmetry groups. There is a suggestion from another study on rats (Nordeen and Yahr, 1982) that the left and right hypothalamus preferentially mediate, respectively, defeminization and masculinization (see chapter 3). In female rats, administering sex hormones to the left side early in life was more likely to result in defeminization (reduced lordosis) in adulthood than the same treatment given to the right side. The opposite pattern was seen for masculinization (mounting behavior)—it was more likely to be increased by right-sided treatment.

Can we generalize from the idea that the left gonad's influence on the left hypothalamus is more likely to influence female reproductive behaviors in a rat, to the mediation of masculine and feminine cognitive

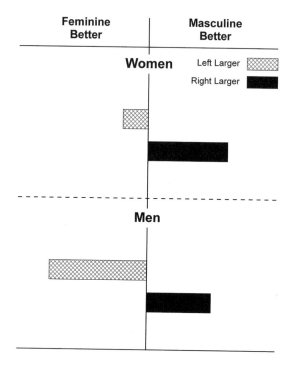

Figure 12.1
Relation between body asymmetry (testicular or breast) and cognitive pattern. People who are larger on the left side tend to do better at "feminine" tasks, whereas those whose right side is larger do better at "masculine" tasks. The graph shows comparisons within each sex, the vertical line representing the mean score for each sex separately.

processes in the brains of humans? We know from findings on neurological patients that two of the male-favoring tests—Mental Rotation and Line Orientation—depend more on the right hemisphere than the left. We have no conclusive information, however, about the brain systems responsible for the other masculine tests, such as Math Reasoning and Throwing Accuracy. For the female-favoring tests used in our study we also have, so far, no information on which neural systems might be critical for their performance. The same is true for the sex-neutral tests.

Nevertheless, the findings encouraged us to think that a link might be found between body asymmetries and brain function. One difficulty with the self-report study described above was that we had no acceptable way of objectively validating the accuracy of subjects' reports of their body asymmetry. So we decided to leave behind that particular method and to look for some other aspect of somatic asymmetry we could investigate objectively.

At about this time I fortuitously came across a report showing that there were generally more ridges on the fingertips of the right hand than the left (Holt, 1968). So we embarked on a project to relate asymmetry in the number of finger ridges (also called dermal ridges) to cognitive function.

Figure 12.2 shows an example of a fingerprint with a loop pattern. There are also patterns with whorls and arches. To get a count of the number of ridges in a loop, a line is drawn from the triradial point on the left of this print to the core point in the center. The ridge count is simply the number of ridges between the two points, in this case, fourteen. The count is generally taken for all five fingers. However, the three middle fingers have a rather high incidence of arch patterns, and arches are arbitrarily given a count of zero by this system. Since the middle fingers

Figure 12.2
Example of a loop fingerprint pattern. A line is drawn from the triradial point at the left to the core point at the right. The ridge count is the number of lines between the triradial and core points. In this case it is 14.

clearly *do* have ridges, we decided to increase the meaningfulness of the numbers by using only counts from the thumb and little finger. We found, when comparing the numbers obtained from two judges in a pretrial, that the possibility of a counting error was approximately one ridge per finger. We therefore decided that a count would only be considered asymmetric if the difference between hands was at least two.

In our first study we took fingerprints from over two hundred right-handed people (as well as a smaller group of left-handers). We found, as had earlier researchers, that men had a higher count overall than women did. This is consistent with the suggestion that the ridge count is inversely related to the amount of material in the sex chromosomes; thus people with an XY makeup (males) have less material and a higher count than those with an XX makeup (females) (Penrose, 1967). We know that this is not simply due to the larger size of men's fingertips because individuals with Turner's syndrome, as a group, have an even higher count than men do. People with Turner's syndrome have only one X, but they are pheno-typically female and have quite small hands. It may be, as Mittwoch (1977) has suggested, that the total ridge count represents the rate of embryonic development at some early stage. Perhaps the less material there is in the sex chromosomes, the faster the cell division can take place.[1]

We also found, as we expected from earlier studies, that most people had a higher count on the right hand than on the left. Both men and women showed the prevailing pattern of a higher right-hand count (R>), and there appeared to be no difference between left-handers and right-handers in this respect. About fifteen to twenty percent of people showed the reverse pattern, a higher count on the left (L>), and of course some showed no difference between hands. As it turned out, more women than men showed the atypical L> pattern. So again we had some evidence that women are more likely than men to show enhanced left-sided growth (as shown in table 12.2).

In another study, one of the most interesting discoveries related finger-ridge patterns to sexual orientation. Jeff Hall's examination of the finger-prints of a fairly large number of homosexual men found that, like heterosexual men, their total ridge count was higher than women's. However, the homosexual males as a group had a higher incidence of the

Table 12.2
Incidence of left-higher finger ridge count in right-handers

	Left>	Left Not>	Total
Women	23	73	96
Men	20	134	154

Note: By a test called "chi square," these frequencies differ at P<.03.

L> asymmetry pattern than straight men did, so in this respect their pattern resembled women's (Hall and Kimura, 1994). Although the homosexual sample also had a higher incidence of left-handers, the difference between homosexual and heterosexual men occurred within the left-handed groups as well, indicating that the finger-ridge pattern was not simply a function of differing hand preference. Recently, a similarly high incidence of the L> pattern has been reported in transsexual males compared to control males (Green, 1998).

Fingerprint patterns appear to be determined by about the fourth fetal month, and apparently do not change after that, unless mechanically altered. There is also known to be a large genetic component to the pattern. So if we find that some human characteristic, behavioral or otherwise, is related to features of the fingerprints, this argues for an early, possible genetic, contribution to the characteristic. In this case, it suggests a prenatal contribution to sexual orientation and to transsexuality in at least some human males.

In our study of fingerprints in heterosexual subjects, we administered more or less the same cognitive tests as we had earlier given to the subjects who estimated their testicular or breast asymmetry. Again, we had masculine, feminine, and neutral tests. In order to have comparable groups, we tried first to get all our L> subjects to return for testing, then matched them in age and program of study with R> subjects. Of course R> subjects far outnumbered the L> subjects, so that not all of the >R group were recalled for cognitive testing.

As in the study on testicular and breast asymmetry, we found that the R> groups were superior on masculine tests and the L> groups superior on feminine tests. Again this was true within each sex, that is, R> women were better than L> women on spatial tests, and the L> women were superior on feminine tests. So in this respect the findings resembled those of the earlier body asymmetry study (figure 12.3).

There was one difference between the studies. On two of the neutral tests (those that do not show sex differences), the R> groups also obtained higher scores than the L> groups did. This was true for the two reasoning tasks—Raven's Matrices, and Inferences—(the latter is a verbal reasoning task). In fact, we might consider the two tests on which there was the largest difference between groups—Mathematical Reasoning and Inferences—to be types of reasoning tasks. These results are shown in figure 12.4.

The fact that intellectual abilities can be related to a physical feature present well before birth of course suggests quite strongly that significant prenatal influences are at work shaping such abilities before any external environmental factors can operate. The fact that most people (and their parents) are quite unaware of their finger ridge patterns, and are certainly unaware of any relation to cognitive function, rules out societal influences for at least a substantial component of these abilities.

Geoff Sanders and his colleagues in England have replicated these findings, not only in adults, but also in children aged eight to nine years (Sanders, Aubert, and Kadam, 1995). They too found that the incidence of a L> count was higher in girls than in boys. In the children, his male-favoring (throwing accuracy) and female-favoring (Purdue Pegboard) tasks were motor tasks, both described in Chapter 4. His findings are depicted in figure 12.5. For adults he employed paper-and-pencil tasks—verbal fluency type tasks for female-favoring, and spatial tasks for male-favoring tests. For both adults and children, he found that those with a L> count (for each sex) performed better on feminine tasks, and those with a R> count performed better on the masculine tasks.

Of course we would like to know more about the brain mechanisms responsible for the differences between these groups. Jeff Hall's research on homosexual men with differing dermal ridge asymmetry showed that his L> group had a smaller right-ear advantage on a dichotic listening-to-words task (Hall and Kimura, 1993) which is usually taken to mean a weaker left-hemisphere lateralization for speech. We wanted to see whether this relationship held true in a heterosexual population, and also to examine more closely the possible contribution of differing commis-

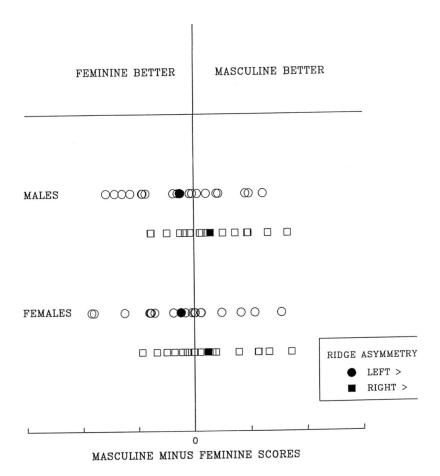

Figure 12.3
Cognitive patterns of people with left-higher or right- higher finger ridge counts. The findings, which are similar to those in figure 12.1, are shown for each subject separately by a circle or square. The mean for each group is shown in solid black. Comparisons are made within each sex, the vertical line representing the mean for each sex separately.

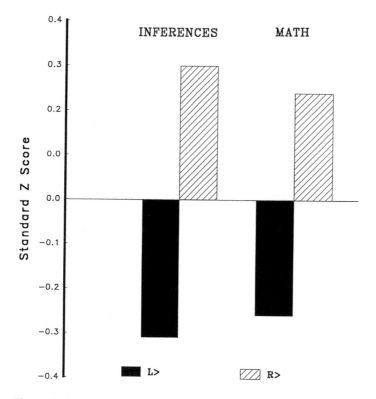

Figure 12.4
Comparison of scores on Mathematical Reasoning and Inferences (a verbal reasoning task) in L> and R> finger-ridge groups. Men and women are combined, and the horizontal line represents the mean for the entire group of subjects.

sural connections in the brains of the two asymmetry groups. The anterior commissure, for example, which begins to develop in the first trimester (Larsen, 1993) is larger in women than in men, and also larger in homosexual men than in heterosexual men (Allen and Gorski, 1992). Could it be that it and/or other commissural pathways differ also between L> and R> persons?

Deborah Saucier and I decided to investigate this possibility. Again, we collected fingerprints from over two hundred undergraduates, then called back all the L> individuals for further testing, nearly all of whom agreed to return. We also called back an equal number of R> persons, matched

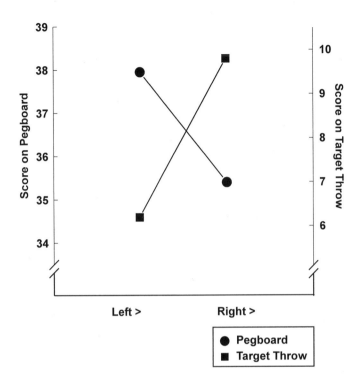

Figure 12.5
Children's scores for the Pegboard and Targeting tasks. The scales for each task
are different but are shown together to contrast the performance of children with
L> and R> ridge counts. (Data from Sanders et al., 1995.)

for age and program of study. We selected approximately equal numbers
of men and women in each group.

Because we were interested in functional brain asymmetry, we administered a variety of perceptual tests known to be sensitive to brain asymmetry, including dichotic listening (presentation of two different words
to the two ears simultaneously), and tachistoscopic tasks (rapid presentation of stimuli to one visual field). The tachistoscopic tests we used were
(1) identification of letters, which usually favors the right visual field
because this input arrives first at the left hemisphere (which is predominant for identification of letters); and (2) dot location, which usually
favors the left field, because this field inputs initially to the right hemi-

sphere (which is predominant for spatial location) (see chapter 10 and figures 10.4 and 10.5).

On dichotic listening, we found the same pattern that Jeff Hall had found with the gay men. That is, although both groups showed the usual right-ear superiority, the L> subjects had a smaller right-ear effect than did the R> subjects, and this was true of both men and women (figure 12.6) (Saucier and Kimura, 1996). We found similar but weaker effects for a letter identification test using a tachistoscope. So there appears to be a tendency for people with a higher ridge count on the left hand to show a weaker left-hemisphere lateralization for speech functions. No significant difference between groups was found for the dot location task.

This finding contradicted the most obvious explanation of our data on cognitive tests—that individuals with a higher left-hand ridge count also had more developed left brain hemispheres. That interpretation would have been consistent with their better fluency, and, some would say, worse spatial ability. But if the left hemisphere had been more developed in L> individuals, we would, if anything, expect a *larger* right-ear advantage rather than the weaker one we consistently got. So it seems likely that there is some other explanation for the smaller right-ear effect, and perhaps also for the different cognitive patterns in L> and R> groups.

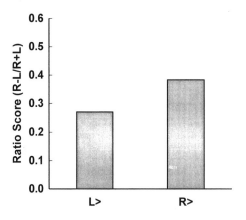

Figure 12.6
Dichotic ear asymmetries in L> and R> groups. The right-ear advantage is usually given as a ratio score, and is smaller in the L> group.

One possible alternative explanation for the weaker right-ear effect might be that L> persons have better connections between the two hemispheres. Note that in the dichotic listening diagram (see figure 10.4), in addition to the pathways shown, there would also be connections between the two hemispheres. Such connections would permit material coming to the left ear, which typically stimulates primarily the right hemisphere, to be relayed from the right to the left hemisphere. We know that everyone has such connections, presumably it is part of the reason we can report left-ear speech sounds at all, since the right hemisphere can't "talk." The stronger these interhemispheric connections are, the more readily information can be sent back and forth between hemispheres. This might enhance left-ear scores and reduce the right-ear advantage for reporting speech sounds. The same principle would operate for letters and words presented to left and right visual fields; that is, the right-field advantage might be reduced in people with better connections between the hemispheres.

To see whether the transmission of information between hemispheres might in fact be different in the two finger-ridge asymmetry groups—L> and R>—we presented tachistoscopically two circles for size comparison. Half the time the circles were in the same visual field (presented to the same hemisphere), and half the time they were in opposite visual fields, so that they would stimulate different hemispheres. We recorded not only whether the response was right or wrong, but also the time it took subjects to make the response. Of course one might expect the response to be slower for everyone when the two circles were presented to different hemispheres than when they came to the same hemisphere, because the information would have to be sent across commissural systems.

We did in fact find evidence for better interhemispheric transmission in the L> group. On the circles-comparison task, the L> group was faster than the R> group when comparing circles presented to different hemispheres; but there was no significant difference between the groups when circles were presented to the same hemisphere (Saucier and Kimura, 1996). This suggests faster transmission of information between hemispheres in the L> ridge count group, and supports the prediction that commissural systems of some kind are better developed in this group.

The reader may be wondering how these strange findings on body asymmetry and cognitive pattern are related to the sex differences we talked about in earlier chapters. We are far from having an answer to this question. It is clear that the cognitive and brain patterns of L> individuals resemble those of average women as compared to men—better fluency, worse math, less asymmetry on dichotic listening, and better interhemispheric connections. The pattern in R> individuals resembles that of average men. Yet, the puzzle is that these differences between body asymmetry groups can be seen in both men and women.

Could it be that L> and R> persons have differing early hormonal environments? Judging by the relation between testosterone levels and performance on "masculine" tasks (chapter 9), we might predict that in men, the R> subjects would have lower T levels than L> subjects. In women, it should be the reverse, that is, we would expect R> subjects to have higher T levels than L> subjects. We have some data on women to suggest that there may be no relation between T levels and direction of finger ridge asymmetry. In men, although the direction of the difference is what we would expect, our sample sizes were too small to make any definitive statement. There is, however, one published study claiming that R> and L> adult males have differing T levels (Jamison, Meier, and Campbell, 1993). Obviously, this is a subject on which we need more research. It is quite possible, however, that hormonal influences are not the primary factors here. There may be other genetic influences, even some that are not directly sex-linked, which contribute to these findings.

Regardless of hormonal status, we have seen a reliable relation between dermal ridge characteristics, which are determined early in fetal life, and performance on certain cognitive and motor tests. This suggests that direction of finger ridge asymmetry is a marker for certain features of nervous system development that occur about the same time as the ridges are developing. Such cognitive functions and their related brain organization must be influenced by events occurring by the end of the fourth fetal month.

Summary

Certain androgenic theories of development have suggested that males may be more developed on the right side of the body, including the brain.

We found that both self-reports of body asymmetry, and objective measures of finger ridge asymmetry showed greater tendencies for rightward growth in men and leftward growth in women. Moreover, the body asymmetry patterns were related to cognitive patterns. Those individuals with leftward asymmetry, whether male or female, tended to perform better than same-sex rightward groups at tasks that generally favor females; whereas those with rightward asymmetry performed better on male-favoring tasks.

Left-hemisphere lateralization for speech also appeared to differ between the two groups. Those with a L> finger ridge count showed lesser left-hemisphere lateralization, that is, weaker right-ear and right-field advantages, than did those with a R> pattern. This argues against the simplistic explanation that the left hemisphere is more developed in the L> groups. Evidence for better interhemispheric transmission in this group suggests, instead, better commissural connections.

Human cognitive patterns and their related brain organization are apparently permanently influenced by physiological events that take place by the fourth fetal month.

Note

1. This suggestion was made by J.A.Y. Hall.

Further Reading

Allen L.S. & Gorski R.A. (1992) Sexual orientation and the size of the anterior commissure in the human brain. *Proceedings of the National Academy of Sciences, 89*, 7199–7202.

Chang K.S.F., Hsu F.K., Chan S.T. & Chan Y.B. (1960) Scrotal asymmetry and handedness. *Journal of Anatomy, 94*, 543–548.

Gerendai I. (1987) Laterality in the neuroendocrine system. In D. Ottoson (Ed.), *Duality and unity of the brain*. London: Macmillan, pp. 17–28.

Geschwind N. & Galaburda A.M. (1985) Cerebral lateralization. Biological mechanisms, associations, and pathology. I. A hypothesis and a program for research. *Archives of Neurology, 42*, 428–459.

Green R. (1998) Introduction to Session II, Sex differences in humans, Symposium on *Estrogen Actions in the Brain*, in honor of Roger Gorski, UCLA, Los Angeles, November, 1998.

Hall J.A. & Kimura D. (1993) Morphological and functional asymmetry in homosexual males. *Society for Neuroscience Abstracts, 19,* 561.

Hall J.A.Y. & Kimura D. (1994) Dermatoglyphic asymmetry and sexual orientation in men. *Behavioral Neuroscience, 108,* 1203–1206.

Holt S.B. (1968) *The genetics of dermal ridges.* Springfield: Charles C. Thomas.

Jamison C.S., Meier R.J. & Campbell B.C. (1993) Dermatoglyphic asymmetry and testosterone levels in normal males. *American Journal of Physical Anthropology, 90,* 185–198.

Kimura D. (1994) Body asymmetry and intellectual pattern. *Personality & Individual Differences, 17,* 53–60.

Kimura D. & Carson M.W. (1995) Dermatoglyphic asymmetry: relation to sex, handedness and cognitive pattern. *Personality & Individual Differences, 19,* 471–478.

Larsen W.J. (1993) *Human embryology.* New York: Churchill Livingstone, chapter 13.

Levy J. & Levy J.M. (1978) Human lateralization from head to foot: sex-related factors. *Science, 200,* 1291–1292.

Mittwoch U. (1988) Ethnic differences in testis size: a possible link with the cytogenetics of true hermaphroditism. *Human Reproduction, 3,* 445–449.

Mittwoch U. (1977) To be right is to be born male. *New Scientist,* 15 January, 74–76.

Mittwoch U. & Mahadevaiah S. (1980) Additional growth—A link between mammalian testes, avian ovaries, gonadal asymmetry in hermaphrodites and the expression of the H-Y antigen. *Growth, 44,* 287–300.

Nordeen E.J. & Yahr P. (1982) Hemispheric asymmetries in the behavioral and hormonal effects of sexually differentiating mammalian brain. *Science, 218,* 391–394.

Penrose L.S. (1967) Finger print pattern and the sex chromosomes. *Lancet,* 11 February, 298–300.

Sanders G., Aubert F. & Kadam A. (1995) Asymmetries in finger ridge count correlate with performance on sexually dimorphic tasks in children and adults. *21st Annual Meeting, International Academy of Sex research,* Provincetown, Mass.

Saucier D.M. & Kimura D. (1996) Dermatoglyphic asymmetry is related to perceptual asymmetry and to interhemispheric transmission. *Laterality, 1,* 185–198.

13

Concluding Remarks

In this book we summarized the main differences in cognitive or problem-solving skills between men and women, and boys and girls, and reviewed the evidence for biological influences on these differences. Currently the most compelling evidence for a biological role is the fact that cognitive patterns are affected by past and current exposure to sex hormones. We also discussed the extent to which certain brain differences may account for the differing cognitive makeup of the sexes, and considered some of the common sociological explanations for sex differences in cognition.

To begin, we recap the story of hormonal contributions to male-favoring abilities. The evidence from persons with early hormonal anomalies such as congenital adrenal hyperplasia (CAH), idiopathic hypogonadotrophic hypogonadism (IHH) and androgen insensitivity indicates that early exposure to androgens contributes significantly to scores on several paper-and-pencil spatial tasks. Similarly, studies of normal young men and women have established that different levels of testosterone are consistently associated with different spatial scores. Fluctuations in sex hormones across seasons or at different phases of the menstrual cycle are also associated with predictable changes in cognitive patterns, including changes in spatial performance.

In addition there is some evidence that math reasoning is related to testosterone levels in men, though perhaps not in women. Finally, although we have as yet no information that hormones influence accuracy of targeting, we have ruled out sports history, male physique, and male "gender" identity as critical factors in producing the sex difference consistently found in this ability.

On female-favoring tasks, we know that fluctuations in estrogen levels are associated with changes in verbal fluency, perceptual speed, and manual dexterity. So far, we have almost no studies relating the reliably found female advantage in verbal memory to levels of sex hormones, though recent reports that taking estrogen therapeutically may enhance memory in older women are suggestive.

Besides sex hormones, we proposed other ways of linking cognitive pattern to prenatal events. Since dermatoglyphic (fingerprint) patterns are fixed early in the second trimester before birth, we can reasonably assume from correlations between aspects of cognitive function and fingerprint characteristics, that there is a prenatal contribution to such functions. In fact, the direction of finger-ridge asymmetry—that is, whether there are more ridges on the left or right hand—is reliably related to whether a person is more likely to show a so-called masculine cognitive pattern or a feminine one, even within a sex. Math reasoning is one ability strongly related to rightward ridge asymmetry, suggesting a prenatal contribution to this math skill. Other abilities which are related to finger-ridge asymmetry include the sexually differentiated motor skills—targeting (rightward asymmetry) and fine motor function (leftward asymmetry). It is a fair assumption that brain systems developing at the same time as the finger ridges are responsible for these effects. At present we don't know whether these brain events are hormonally linked.

Of course, differences in behavior between individuals or groups must in some way be mediated by the nervous system. Much is known in rodents about the effect of hormones on brain structure and function. We know, for example, a fair amount about how the hypothalamus mediates sexual behavior, about the hormonal mechanism in the amygdala's mediation of rough-and-tumble play, and about the role of the hippocampal complex in certain spatial maze-solving functions. We can manipulate hormones in nonhumans and look at the effects on brain and behavior as we cannot do in people. Such experiments provide us with very useful models of how similar functions may operate in people, though ultimately these ideas must somehow be tested on humans.

Several contrasts in human brain structure and function between the sexes were described, with special reference to commissural systems, anterior-posterior function, and left-right lateralization of function. Although we would expect such brain differences to be related to differences in human cognitive patterns, we have up to now had little in the way of solid evidence linking sex variations in brain organization to cognitive abilities. The absence of such evidence is most likely due to the difficulty of collecting it. Some of the best information we have about the functions of particular brain regions comes from persons with neurological damage. Most studies of this kind, however, have not compared men and women—perhaps in part because larger numbers of patients would be needed to make such a comparison.

The widely held assumption that there are major differences in the degree of brain lateralization of function between men and women is debatable. Even where sex differences in brain lateralization clearly exist, no convincing case has yet been made that they influence cognitive pattern. Nonetheless, it is likely that in the near future new brain-imaging techniques will help uncover relationships between individual brain organization and cognitive abilities.

Taking all these facts together, we can say with certainty that there are substantial stable sex differences in cognitive functions like spatial rotation ability, mathematical reasoning, and verbal memory; and in motor skills requiring accurate targeting and finger dexterity. We can also state with certainty that most of these sexually differentiated functions are strongly influenced by early and/or current hormonal environments. Other factors may contribute to these abilities prenatally through nonhormonal mechanisms.

Evidence for socialization influences on such differences between the sexes is meagre, and most often focuses on relating past life experience (preferred sports, school courses taken, presumed parental influence) to current abilities. All such associations are of course open to alternative interpretations. Some people have also claimed that cognitive sex differences have been declining, implying that as men's and women's environments become more alike, they will differ less. We pointed out other reasons for reduced sex differences, when they occur, including the changing of test items to favor one group (typically females). Often the arguments for socializing influences consist in simply insisting that such explanations be given priority.

What evidence we have does not suggest that the male superiority on imaginal rotation and mathematical reasoning has declined over the last few decades. The very early appearance in life of sex differences in imaginal rotation ability and in certain motor skills is probably more easily reconcilable with pre- and perinatal biological influences than with gendered socialization. However, it must also be said that "natural experiments" relevant to socializing influences are less likely to occur than those relevant to the role of sex hormones. The effect of sex-of-rearing in persons with anomalous genital structure, for example, has simply not been sufficiently studied.

How Valid Are Tests?

Keep in mind that many of the tests that demonstrate consistent sex differences, are employed in research for that very reason. That is, they are probably relatively "pure" ability tests, meaning that they have minor overlap with other tests. However, in the world outside the laboratory, most of our activities involve a mix of abilities. This means, potentially, that performance on pure tests may not predict performance very well on a variety of real-world activities. For example, finding one's around way in a relatively familiar geographical area, which would allow the use of both geometric and landmark strategies, may not necessarily reveal a male superiority.

Similarly, an everyday motor activity, such as driving a car, combines both precise intrapersonal activities (changing gears, using the steering wheel) with extrapersonal activities (judging the distance and speed of other vehicles). The more mixed an activity, the less likely it is that any one psychometric test will predict performance on it. Even occupations that are quite demanding of spatial ability, such as some branches of engineering or architecture, will also require other general skills, such as organizing one's sequence of behaviors, setting priorities, collating information from various sources, and so forth. The likelihood of success in an occupation or profession is determined by a multitude of intellectual and motivational factors, not merely by performance on relatively pure psychometric tests. So we should not interpret even large and consistent sex differences on any one test as indicating that only men can be rocket scientists, or only women can be homemakers.

Moreover, most of the tests we discussed in this book are time-limited. That is, they contain too many items for most people to complete in the time allowed. Unquestionably, if unlimited time were given, men's and women's scores on some tasks would approach or equal each other. Some have argued that speed-of-processing should be irrelevant because in the real world we do not have such strict time limits, which give males an unfair advantage. Others argue just as strongly that, on the contrary, the speed with which a cognitive task can be done is an intrinsic component of that ability. We know, for example that there is a fairly strong relationship between speed-of-processing on a complex reaction-time task, and overall IQ, suggesting that the speed element is pertinent to performance on intelligence tests (Jensen, 1982; Vernon, 1983). One study of a mental rotation test found that although giving unlimited time reduced the score difference between gifted teenage boys and girls, it did not eliminate it (Gallagher and Johnson, 1992). The authors nevertheless concluded that they had helped "dispel the myth that girls are less able than boys in . . . spatial ability."

You may be asking why we should care about studies on sex differences in cognitive function. What if women don't on average score as high as men on certain math and spatial tests. What if men on average don't do as well as women on verbal memory or certain fluency tasks? Is this really relevant or important to our daily lives? For the most part, the answer may be that it isn't. We don't make our life choices on the basis of what the average man or woman does, we make them on the basis of our own talents, interests, and background. As long as opportunities are available to men and women equally, and selections and decisions are made on the basis of objective and appropriate criteria, the fact of average sex differences may be irrelevant. The chief value of studying sex differences, from a scientific point of view, is that it provides a fruitful method for understanding how differing cognitive patterns arise. It is one important way of learning more about ourselves as human beings.

However, not everyone agrees that admission to occupations or to academic programs should be objectively based, and it must also be said that the grounds on which people are admitted to some occupations sometimes appear irrelevant. For example, the requirement of a college degree for many jobs is often really an employer's lazy way of screening for intelligence. Questioning and scrutinizing the criteria traditionally employed for access to education and employment may be a healthy attitude. On the other hand, it is also pointless to deny that natural differences in talents or interests do exist across individuals and groups; and that those differences help determine representation in certain professions and occupations.

Some people believe that knowing more about sex differences in abilities will put women at a special disadvantage, since it is currently true that the largest established differences we know about favor men. Radical feminists are prone to the view that knowledge of sex differences should be suppressed. They suggest that the lower representation of women in the sciences, especially the physical sciences and mathematics, is due primarily to the tendency to "gender" occupations. They feel that accepting the reality of certain sex differences in cognitive function provides an excuse for keeping women out of science and math fields, notwithstanding the explanations for the smaller numbers of women in the physical sciences we discussed in chapter 6.

Some people have argued that the gendering of science, and hence the disadvantaging of women begins early, in high school or before. Their solution is to encourage women to take more science and math courses, so that they later qualify for positions in related fields. Simple encouragement, of course, is not a bad thing; but if it takes the form of making people act out of a sense of duty, or causes them to feel guilty about their life choices, we must question the use, and the ethics, of such pressures. Lubinski and Benbow (1992) report that even the girls in their highly math-talented samples often had more person-oriented interests than did the boys, so that they might not enter fields in which math is critical. It is begging the question to insist that their choices are mostly due to societal influences.

It's doubtful there is any good evidence that women are currently being kept out of science or other fields by unfair testing. Admission to most academic programs is based largely on course grades and on aptitude test scores. Women apply to advanced training in engineering, physics, and mathematics in much smaller numbers than do men. They typically take fewer relevant science courses. It is hard to believe, in our determinedly egalitarian society, that anyone on an admissions committee (which has access to all candidates' scores) would be inclined to suggest that women not be admitted on the same basis as men merely because they *believe* them to be worse on math! On the contrary, just the reverse is likely to occur—women are likely be admitted because a particular discipline feels it should have more women. If in fact individuals are admitted to programs on the basis of their actual past performance, we cannot regard this as discrimination against women; it is simply the application of consistent standards for everyone.

Unfortunately, many people confuse equality of opportunity or access with equality of *outcome*. It may turn out that the most objective, most appropriate and fairest criteria for admission to a program or an occupation will favor men in some cases and women in others. This in fact is to be expected if the ability differences described in this book are as stable as most seem to be. Tinkering with existing aptitude tests in such a way as to produce equal scores between groups such as men and women, or between ethnic groups, is of course quite possible. Whether it is legitimate, in terms of the ultimate aims of aptitude tests, is another matter. For example, it has been claimed that the National Merit Scholarship Program in the United States has engaged in "gender gerrymandering" in its use of the PSAT (a junior version of the SAT) as a criterion. The selection index of the program is "two times the verbal score plus the mathematics score," which was apparently adopted to "try and compensate for girls' math scores by counting the verbal score twice and the math score only once" (Murray, 1997).

An alternative method of achieving the same end is to pad the criterion with more tests that girls do as well or better than boys do. A recent attempt to do this involved adding a "writing skills" subtest to the PSAT. However, the slight advantage for girls on this test was not enough to offset the boys advantage on math, the section of the PSAT showing the largest sex difference (Arenson, 1998). Clearly the aim of such maneuvers is to achieve a state in which males' and females' overall scores, or criterion scores, are equal. Only then will the scores be considered "unbiased." Whether they will any longer be predictive of success in fields such as science is, to some advocacy groups, irrelevant.

Consider what may seem far-fetched, but is a sadly possible scenario:

A job requires as a major part of its activity that heavy bags of sand be carried some distance. The personnel manager has used as one test for the job, a measure of how heavy an iron weight an applicant can lift. A woman has applied and is unable to meet this criterion. She complains to an office of civil rights that the test is discriminatory, because very few women can meet the requirement. The company is told that it must employ a test that will admit equal numbers of women and men. Consequently, they decide to administer a pegboard task, of the kind described in chapter 4, which measures finger dexterity. Women perform at least as well on this test as do men. You can fill in the rest. There is in principle no difference between this imaginary situation, and one that special interest groups currently attempt to create by manipulating tests of intellectual ability. While we are perhaps not quite as certain that math is as necessary for study in the physical sciences, as that a minimum of strength is needed to carry sandbags, the parallel is very close.

Even when average differences between groups are small, they can allow us to make predictions about groups as a whole. For some occupations, for example, it may be that the decisive scores are those at the top end of the distribution, not those in the average range. At the same time we must keep in mind that a prediction about what any *one* person will score on a particular test—if we know only the person's sex—will be poor, even when group differences between the sexes are large. So what is valid for the group need not apply to an individual. Each person's intellectual makeup, being the intersection of neural, genetic, hormonal, and environmental influences, is unique. Equity requires treating each person as an individual, not as a member of a group.

Further Reading

Arenson K. (1998) Test gap between sexes narrows. *Toronto Globe and Mail*, 15 January, p. A15.

Gallagher S.A. & Johnson E.S. (1992) The effect of time limits on performance of mental rotations by gifted adolescents. *Gifted Child Quarterly*, 36, 19–22. (Quotation from page 183)

Jensen A.R. (1982) Reaction time and psychometric *g*. In H.J. Eysenck (Ed.), *A model for intelligence*. New York: Springer, pp. 93–132.

Lubinski D. & Benbow C.P. (1992) Gender differences in abilities and preferences among the gifted: implications for the math-science pipeline. *Current Directions in Psychological Science*, *1*, 61–66.

Murray D. (1997) Letter to *Academic Questions*, *10*, Spring, 7–8.

Vernon P.A. (1983) Speed of information processing and general intelligence. *Intelligence*, *7*, 53–70.

Appendix
Dealing with Numbers

Because we often refer to studies which compare groups of different people (in this book, usually males and females), it is useful to know how social scientists go about drawing conclusions from such comparisons. Most of the abilities we have talked about have what in statistics is called a *normal distribution*. This means that if you made a graph of the number of people who receive each score on a given test, you would produce a shape something like a bell (the *bell curve*), with the most-frequently occurring score (called the *mode*) at the peak or top of the bell (figure A.1). When we have large numbers of test-takers the mode usually coincides with the *mean*, or average score. Scores above and below the mode or mean are less and less frequent as you go out to the extremes, that is, not many people have very high or very low scores.

Differences between Groups

When we compare two groups, we usually deal only with a small portion of the population we are investigating. Let's say that our interest is in left-handers and right-handers. For some reason we want to know whether these two kinds of people differ in some way, perhaps on a particular spatial task. The ideal way to determine this would be to test the entire population, that is, all the left-handers and all the right-handers in the world; we could then be certain that we were getting an accurate picture of how the two groups perform. This is, of course, nearly always impossible. So instead we test what is called a *random sample*, that is, a small number of persons from each group chosen in an unbiased way. To ensure that this sample is really representative of the groups as a whole,

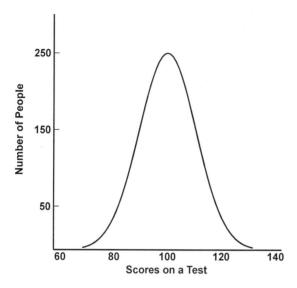

Figure A.1
Normal or "bell" curve. This graph shows a hypothetical plot of the number of people obtaining each score on a test.

we try to solicit people for our study in a way that is equivalent in the two groups. For example, if we obtained our left-handers from a left-handers club, joined by people from all walks of life, and got our right-handers from an undergraduate student population, we would not have used equivalent selection methods. We could probably not legitimately compare the two groups.

This seems obvious, but there are some occasions when selection factors operate that we may not have known about or predicted. Let's say we approach a group or organization to solicit left-handed and right-handed subjects (the human objects of investigations are called subjects or participants). We explain that we are going to give them some tests, including a spatial test. Some of the left-handers might conceivably be reluctant to take any tests; they may have been told that they are "klutzes" (because of a little awkwardness in dealing with a right-handed world). So they don't volunteer for the study. Let's suppose that these particular left-handers would have scored poorly on the spatial test if they had taken it. The result might be that the left-handers who *do* volunteer obtain higher scores than the right-handers, because the low-scoring segment of left-handers has not taken part. The average or mean scores of the left-handers and right-handers might be different but only because we didn't have a representative sample of left-handers.

Alternatively, the left-handed "klutzes" (who didn't volunteer) might actually have scored above average, had they taken the test. In that case, the left-handers who do come into the study might get a lower score than the right-handers because the top-scoring left-handers are not included. Again we would have a nonrepresentative sample of left-handers. So you can see that there are many pitfalls in choosing subjects for a study, and that we need to know as much as possible about how the subjects in any study were recruited. For the same reason, experimenters like to repeat or *replicate* their findings. If they get the same results in two or three studies, there is a better chance that the findings are reliable.

Probability

When we say that two groups differ *significantly* on a measure, we actually mean that we have gone through a mathematical process that allows us to reject the possibility that the two samples come from the same hypothetical population as far as this measure is concerned. The conventional assumption is that there is no difference, which is called the *null hypothesis*. This perverse statistical hypothesis says that any apparent difference between the means of two samples is due to chance selection from a single large population, that there really is no reliable difference between the groups. So the procedure for testing the difference actually tests whether we have sufficient evidence to reject the null hypothesis.

Rejection of the null hypothesis (or acceptance of a real difference) is usually reported as a probability statement. You may read that the probability of the difference between two means is less than .05. This means that the chance that the two groups come from the same population (hence, do not differ) is less than one in twenty. If the probability is less than .01, the chance is less than one in a hundred. Obviously, the lower the probability, the higher the reliability of the difference.

How is this probability calculated? We will not actually do the calculations, but we will discuss factors that go into the equation and thus contribute to the decision. One important factor is the size of each sample. Let's suppose, continuing with the example of left-handers and right-handers, that we have tested three left-handers and four right-handers. The first thing we might do is to calculate the mean, or average score for each group. If the left-handers' scores are 11, 13, and 18, and the right-handers' are 11, 13, 14, and 15, the mean for the former is 14.0, and for the latter is 13.25. The mean score for left-handers is higher, but there is a fair amount of overlap between the groups. One left-hander in particular has a high score, whereas the other two average less than the right-handers, so we may also wonder how stable a picture we have. Let's suppose that we add another ten people to each group, and now the two averages are 13.7 and 13.4, much closer to each other.

We see here the difficulty of small sample sizes, in that we are more likely to have an unrepresentative or unstable picture of a group's average score when the numbers are small. If we had thirty left-handers and forty right-handers, assuming we have chosen them equivalently, we would have more confidence in the stability of the mean scores. If we had three hundred and four hundred, respectively (an unlikely situation), we would be even more confident. This illustrates the fact that the size of the sample is an important component in calculating the probability that two groups differ significantly.

Variation

Another factor that enters into the calculation is the variation in scores that we see within each group. If there had been no extreme scores in our earlier example of three left-handers and four right-handers, we might have been more willing to accept the scores as representative. In fact, if we had had the unusual situation in which there was no overlap between the groups, we would have been fairly confident that the two groups differed. For example, suppose that the three left-handers had scores of 16, 17, and 18, and the right-handers had scores of 11, 13, 13, and 14. The variation within each group would be less than before.

We can illustrate this further by going back to our "normal" curve. Figure A.2 shows examples of two different situations. In both top and bottom figures, the mean score of the left-handers is the same (just under

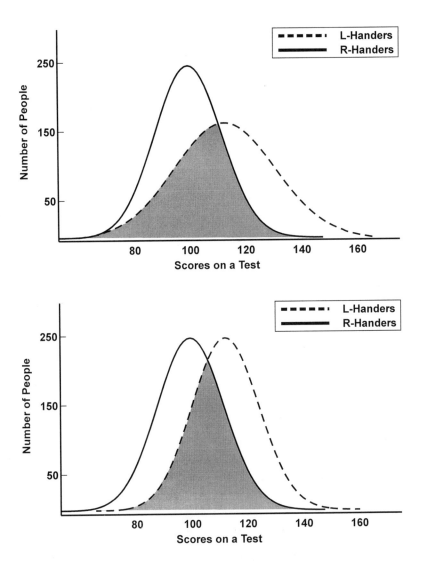

Figure A.2
How variation in scores *within* a group affects comparisons. The overlap (shaded area) in scores between left-handers and right-handers is greater in the top diagram, where the left-handers show more variation then they do in the bottom diagram.

120), as is the mean score of the right-handers (100). But in one comparison, the variation in the scores of the left-handers is larger than in the other. As you can see, even though the differences between the group means are the same, the overlap in scores (shaded area) between groups is smaller in one case (bottom graph) than the other (top graph). Greater overlap means that the groups are more likely to come from the same population, and thus are less likely to be "significantly different" statistically. Clearly, then, it is important to have some measure of variation within a group if we are to evaluate the significance of a difference.

The most common measure of variation within a group is called the *standard deviation*, abbreviated as *SD*. Its calculation depends, in principle, on taking each individual score in the group, subtracting the group's mean score from it, adding up all these differences, and dividing by the total sample size. This gives us, roughly, the average deviation of the scores from the mean. (Actual SD calculation is a bit more complex.) *The more scores there are that are farther from the mean, the larger the SD.* If most scores are near the mean, the SD will be smaller. The smaller the variation within the groups being compared, the greater is the "significance" of the difference between groups.

In fact, it is quite common to express the difference between two groups in terms of how different they are, relative to their averaged standard deviations. To do this, the difference between groups is divided by the standard deviation. Assuming roughly comparable SDs in each group, we can ask, by how many SDs do they differ? Figure A.3 shows two examples. One (bottom graph) is a comparison in which the two groups differ by one full SD, a very large difference, in practice. This is called an *"effect size"* of 1.0. When two groups differ by 1 SD, about 84 percent of the people in one group fall below the mean of the other group. The other example (top graph) shows a difference of 0.3 SD, or an effect size of 0.3. While it could still be significant statistically, especially with a large sample size, it would be of less practical or predictive significance.

Correlation

Another important question we often ask in discussing human abilities is how one characteristic is related to another. Implicit in this question often

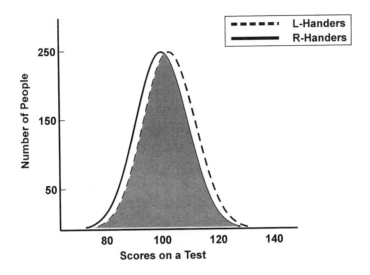

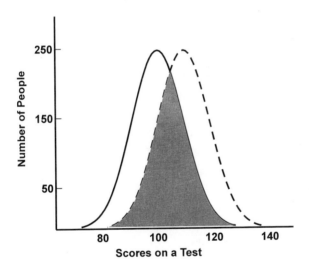

Figure A.3
Differences between groups as a function of the standard deviation. In the top diagram, the difference is 0.3 SD, whereas in the bottom it is a full 1.0 SD.

is an assumption of causality, that is, that one characteristic causes the other. But as we shall see, such assumptions about the cause of a relationship are often wrong. Take the example of height and weight. These two characteristics are *positively* related, meaning that across many people, as one measure gets larger, so does the other. The relation between two such variables can be measured by a *correlation coefficient*. A perfect correlation is represented by the number 1, which is the highest correlation possible. This would mean that if we arrayed the values for height and weight across our subjects, the tallest person would also be the heaviest, the next tallest the next heaviest, and so on, to the shortest who would be the lightest. Perfect correlations are rare, and since we know that some tall people are lighter than some short people, we would not expect a perfect correlation. In fact, the correlation between these two variables in one North American sample is about .70, which is still very high.

A zero correlation means that there is no relation between two variables. Correlations between various parts of a standard IQ test range from .40 to .70. Correlation coefficients, like other statistical values, may be judged significant or not, depending not only on their magnitude, but also on the size of the sample they are calculated from. When we say that a correlation is significant, we mean that there is a low probability of its actually being zero in the total population.

We can also find a *negative* correlation. For example, in men there is a negative correlation between age and amount of hair, reflecting the fact that as men age they have less hair. Such a negative correlation is as meaningful as a positive one, but it indicates that the relationship is inverse. A perfect negative correlation is represented by −1.

An important thing to remember about correlations is that they tell us that two things are related, but they cannot in themselves indicate *how* they are related, that is, what the nature of the relationship is. Because some correlations clearly do represent causal directional relations, we can be fooled into thinking that other correlations do the same. We know that as you increase height, all other things being equal, weight must increase, so it is clear that *part* of the relation between height and weight is caused by this fact. But in most correlations, we are not entitled to infer that changes in one variable cause changes in the other.

A popular example will make this clear. We would probably find, if we investigated, that there is a significant correlation between episodes of eating ice cream cones and sunburn. That is, if we had people keep a record each week for fifty-two weeks, how many times they ate an ice-cream cone or had sunburn, we would find, across many individuals, that as one went up, so would the other. Docs this mean that eating ice cream cones causes sunburn? Of course not. Or that getting sunburn causes you to eat ice cream cones? Again the answer is no. The relationship is presumably mediated by the fact that during the summer, when it's warm and sunny, people are more likely to experience both of these things. So the causal basis of the relationship is something else, a third factor (the hot sunny summer) that was not measured.

Here is another example. Let's say that over a certain specified span of years (e.g., 1960–1980), violent crimes increased. Let's also assume that during the same period, the frequency of violence on TV shows increased. If we plot the two frequencies each year over the twenty-year period, we might find a significant positive correlation. What does this mean? It could mean that watching violent episodes on TV leads people to commit a greater number of violent crimes. Or it could mean that when violent crimes increase in the real world, depiction of violence also increases on TV. Or there might be other more complex relationships: for example, that the number of people in the age range in which most violent crime occurs (late teens and early twenties) increased during this period, and that this age group also prefers to watch more violence on TV. You can probably come up with other possible connections.

Now how might this ambiguity apply to correlations involved with abilities? A common observation on sex differences is that boys and girls have different experiences while growing up. Therefore, when we see that they also have different kinds of abilities as adults, we tend to infer that the differing childhood experiences were the cause. And indeed this may sometimes be correct, though it is far from being an infallible rule. Let's say we are trying to understand how the differences in certain math scores between men and women come about. Some of the studies on this topic find significant correlations between number of math courses taken, and scores on math aptitude tests, and they conclude that the former determine the latter.

But we could just as easily argue that if you have a strong aptitude for math, it will lead you to take more math courses. The correlation in itself does not allow us to say how these two things are related. Similarly, if we found that there was a correlation between whether parents like math, and their children's scores on math tests, this would still leave the question about causal relation unanswered. Is it that some parents are encouraging their children more? Or is it that the parents have an above-average aptitude for math that is genetically transmitted to the children? Or even, is it possible that because the children have high math aptitude, their parents have a positive attitude toward the subject? These are all logical possibilities.

These limitations of correlational data must constantly be kept in mind. We need to know more than the fact that two things are correlated, in order to accurately ascribe causality. Usually, we do have other information that helps us select the most probable explanation. In science, the rule-of-thumb is to give more credence to explanations that best fit all the available facts, and that are also consistent with a broad base of knowledge. To *prove* a particular point of view beyond any doubt is almost impossible, because it would mean ruling out all possible alternative explanations, including some not yet devised. It is much easier to disprove inaccurate explanations than to prove accurate ones. The best we can do is make a particular explanation more and more likely, by accumulating additional evidence in its favor, and finding none that clearly refute it.

Factor Analysis

Correlation is also useful for determining how two different abilities are related. For example, it is often claimed that spatial ability and mathematical ability are highly related, more so than other kinds of abilities. If that were true, we should consistently see quite high correlations between scores on tests of these two abilities. In fact, data from one of our studies do not support that claim: we didn't find that scores on a math reasoning test correlated any better with spatial tests than they did with a test of vocabulary. (This is discussed further in chapter 6.)

We could ask even broader questions about how abilities are related—for example, how many *different* abilities are there? Some researchers might say only two- verbal abilities and nonverbal abilities. Others might claim a dozen or more distinctively different abilities. One way to approach this question is to administer a wide variety of tests of ability to a large group of people, and then calculate correlations among the scores on the tests. Some subgroups of tests will have high correlations with each other, thus forming clusters of abilities, or *factors* as they are called. Abilities like spatial mental rotation will generally show fairly high correlations with other spatial tests, but they may not correlate highly with tests such as verbal memory. The method, called *factor analysis*, tells us something about how specific cognitive abilities relate to other specific abilities.

Most tests of cognitive ability, however, show some degree of relation to all the other tests. This fact has suggested to people researching the nature of intelligence that, in addition to the specific abilities which we emphasized in this book, there is some general factor in intelligence, called the *g* factor for short. This factor is assumed to contribute to all or most tests of cognitive function, however different they may appear to be (Seligman, 1992).

Summary

When we compare two groups of people on anything, we can almost never compare the entire population defined by the groups. So what we do instead is to take a *sample* of individuals from each group, which we intend to be representative of that group. Obviously, if the way we have chosen one group differs from the way we have chosen the comparison group, we may not have a valid study.

However we choose our groups, we will almost never have identical average scores for the two. Just by chance, there is a high probability that the two mean scores will differ by a small or a large amount. We therefore have to have a method for deciding whether the difference we found between our sample groups really holds for the populations they represent, or whether it could have occurred by chance. In making this calculation, we take into account not only the size of the mean difference, but also the size of the samples, and the variation of scores within each sample. Variation is usually measured by the *standard deviation*.

We also often want to know whether two different human characteristics are related (e.g., height and sports participation). We might also want to know how various cognitive abilities are related to each other. A common way to look at such relationships is to use *correlations*. The *correlation coefficient* ranges from zero to one, with 1.0 representing a perfect correlation. A logical error people often make is to assume that if two things are correlated, one causes the other. But this is by no means always the case, and we must be very careful in making inferences from correlations.

Further Reading

Seligman D. (1992) *A question of intelligence. The IQ debate in America.* New York: Birch Lane Press. (Especially chapter 2)

Glossary

Activational The immediate or current effects of hormones, as compared to their early prenatal and perinatal **organizing** effects.

Alpha-fetoprotein A protein present in newborn rodents which binds to estrogen, and is thought to be the means by which females are protected from **defeminization** and **masculinization**.

Amygdala Part of the limbic system of the brain that plays an important role in fear and aggression, and that apparently mediates rough-and-tumble play.

Androgen-insensitivity syndrome Sometimes called *testicular feminization* syndrome, a condition in XY individuals in which androgens are produced but there are no, or not sufficient, androgen receptors in the body cells, rendering the androgens ineffective. The individual's **phenotype** is female.

Androgens Masculinizing hormones, including **testosterone, dihydrotestosterone,** and **androstenedione,** produced primarily by the testes, but also by adrenal glands and ovaries.

Androstenedione An androgen produced by the adrenal glands.

Anterior Referring to the front (e.g., of the brain).

Anterior commissure A small **commissure** shown to be sexually dimorphic; it also differs in size between homosexual and heterosexual men.

Aphasia A disorder in speaking resulting from damage to the brain, usually the left hemisphere.

Apraxia A difficulty in performing specified movements on command or by imitation, despite good strength and motility; it usually results from left-hemisphere damage.

Aptitude tests Tests aimed at measuring an individual's basic potential for certain spheres of ability. Differentiating them from achievement tests, the problems posed require only the basic knowledge that most people would have at that age or school level.

Aromatase An enzyme that converts **testosterone** to **estradiol.**

Aromatization The process of converting **testosterone** to **estradiol** by means of the enzyme **aromatase.**

Benton Line Orientation   A test on which a series of two lines of differing slopes are presented, and matched to those from a large array of lines.

Binocular disparity   The fact that the two eyes, because of their different positions in the head, do not receive exactly identical visual images from the external world; an important cue to depth.

Castration   Removal of **testes**, leaving penis intact.

Circadian   Referring to a daily (24-hour) cycle.

Commissures   Connections between the two cerebral hemispheres; includes **corpus callosum, anterior commissure,** and so forth.

Congenital adrenal hyperplasia (CAH)   A condition in which the adrenal glands produce an excess of androgens, due indirectly to a defect in the production of cortisol.

Corpus callosum   the largest bundle of fibers connecting the two cerebral hemispheres; the major **commissure.**

Correlation coefficient   A measure of the degree to which two variables are associated in the same people; ranges from -1.0 (a perfect negative correlation) through zero (no correlation) to $+1.0$ (a perfect positive correlation).

Defeminization   The early organizational process in male mammals under the influence of sex hormones, by which "default" female sexual behaviors (e.g., **lordosis**) are suppressed, and will normally not occur in adulthood.

Dendrite   The receiving end of a neuron or nerve cell; usually it has many branches.

Dermatoglyphics   The study of fingerprints.

Dichotic listening   A **perceptual asymmetry** technique in which two different sounds are presented to the two ears simultaneously.

Digit span   The longest series of orally presented digits a person can repeat back.

Digit Symbol test   A test on which the digits 1 to 9 are each paired with a symbol; subjects must fill in the appropriate symbols on a sheet containing a large series of the digits. In the converse version (called the **Symbol Digit** test), the digits must be filled in instead of the symbols.

Dihydrotestosterone   An **androgen** converted from **testosterone** by the action of the enzyme **5-alpha-reductase.**

Disembedding   Recognizing a shape although it is embedded or hidden in a complex surround.

Double blind   A procedure in which neither the experimenter nor the subject of the research knows whether a real or a pseudo-treatment is being given; common in drug studies.

Effect size   The difference between two means expressed, not in absolute terms, but in terms of their **standard deviations (SDs)**. An effect size of 1 means that the two means in question differ by one full standard deviation (SDs are pooled for this calculation).

Estradiol An estrogen important for the activation of female reproductive behavior, but that also takes part in the organization of male behaviors early in life.

Factor analysis A **correlational** technique in which a number of measures of abilities are taken and the researcher looks for clusters of abilities, that is, abilities that correlate highly with one another. Such clusters are called factors.

Field independence The ability to ignore a distracting surrounding to solve a problem; for example in **disembedding** or in identifying the true vertical within a tilted frame as in the **Rod-and-Frame** test.

Finger ridge count (also dermal ridge count) A measure of the number of ridges or lines on a fingerprint pattern, usually taken for all 5 fingers of each hand. It has a large genetic component.

5-alpha-reductase An enzyme that converts **testosterone** to **dihydrotestosterone**.

Functional magnetic resonance imaging (fMRI) A technique that measures the activity of various brain regions by detecting the amount of oxygen carried in the bloodstream, which affects its magnetic properties.

Flutamide A substance that blocks or takes up androgen receptors so that **androgens** cannot act on them; thus an anti-androgen.

Functional asymmetry Refers to the greater dependence on one or the other brain hemisphere of various behavioral functions; for example, speech is generally dependent on the left hemisphere.

***g* factor** An hypothesized general factor in cognitive tests representing an underlying basic intelligence factor.

Gonads Organs (**testes** in males, **ovaries** in females) that produce reproductive cells (sperm in males and eggs in females) and sex-appropriate mixes of hormones.

Hippocampus A structure in the most medial portion of the temporal lobe that appears to have important memory functions, and in nonhumans, perhaps specifically spatial memory functions.

Hominid man and the fossil ancestors of man.

Hunter-gatherer A term used to refer to a way of life prevalent through most of hominid evolution, in which food was obtained by a combination of hunting (animal) and gathering (vegetable) material. The division of labor is assumed to have been primarily hunting or scavenging by males and gathering by females.

Hypothalamus A clump of nuclei at the base of the brain; a control center for basic functions such as eating, drinking, temperature regulation, reproductive behavior, and hormone secretion.

Idiopathic hypogonadotrophic hypogonadism (IHH) A condition in which there is a deficiency in the gonadotrophic hormones which regulate production and release of sex hormones; in men the result is abnormally low levels of **testosterone** and small genitals.

INAH (Interstitial nuclei of the anterior hypothalamus) portions of this group of nuclei are thought to be the human analogue of the **SDN-POA** in rodents.

Incidental memory   Memory for material in the absence of any instructions to recall it.

Interception test   A test of the accuracy in intercepting a moving object.

Interhemispheric transmission   Transfer of information between cerebral hemispheres, presumably via **commissural** systems.

Landmarks   Items in the environment that may be used to navigate through space.

Lordosis   A stereotyped reproductive behavior seen in female rats whereby the back is arched and the tail diverted to facilitate penetration by the male's penis.

Manual sequence box   An apparatus upon which a series of hand movements must be performed as quickly as possible, as a test of manual skill.

Masculinization   An **organizational** process in young male mammals under the direction of sex hormones, in which the reproductive behaviors of mounting, penetration by the penis, and ejaculation, are facilitated so that they occur (with appropriate hormonal priming) later in adulthood. Also used to refer to the organization of nonreproductive behaviors.

Mean   The average of a series of measures.

Mental (imaginal) rotation   Solving a problem by imagining how an object would look when rotated in some way.

Meta-analysis   Analysis of the findings across many related studies.

Mode   The most frequently occurring score in a series of scores on any measure; with large samples of people, the mode usually coincides with the **mean**.

Mounting   A typically male reproductive behavior in which, prior to penetration, the male's forelegs grasp the female around the body while he mounts her from behind.

Müllerian ducts   Embryonic ducts that have the potential to form part of the female internal reproductive system, the uterus and Fallopian tubes.

Müllerian regression factor (MRF)   A substance secreted by the embryonic **testes** that dissolves the Müllerian tubes.

Natural selection   An evolutionary process whereby the genetic constitution of a species is gradually determined by environment factors; those characteristics that promote survival are passed on to the offspring.

Neurotransmitter   A chemical released by the sending end, or axon, of a neuron; it diffuses across the axon-dendrite junction (synapse), to act on the **dendrite** of the receiving cell. Major neurotransmitters are norepinephrine, dopamine, serotonin, and acetylcholine.

Normal curve   The bell-shaped curve that results when we plot the scores for many human cognitive tests.

Organizational   The long-term often irreversible effects of sex hormones on the early nervous system and on related behaviors, especially well studied in mammals. Organizational effects are usually limited in efficacy to a critical period before or just after birth. For some behaviors, current **activational** effects in adulthood are also needed.

Ovaries   The female **gonads** contained in the abdominal cavity;

Perceptual asymmetry   The fact that input to the two ears or two visual fields is not processed symmetrically. The difference between left and right ears or visual fields is related to whether material presented is verbal or nonverbal and thus, which brain hemisphere does the major processing. Ear- or visual-field advantages are assumed to reflect the functioning of the opposite hemisphere.

Perceptual speed   The rapid comparison of stimuli or groups of stimuli to determine which are identical matches.

PET (positron emission tomography)   A method for imaging the activity of the brain which depends on the brain's absorbing more glucose in more active regions; the glucose uptake is detected by an attached radioisotope.

Phenotype   The actual appearance of an individual, regardless of genetic makeup; to be distinguished from genotype, the genetic constitution.

Placebo   A pseudo-treatment given to research subjects for comparison with an actual treatment. For example, one group may be given a pill containing a real drug and another a pill that has no active ingredients, the placebo.

Planum temporale   A region of the temporal lobe on the superior surface, behind the auditory cortex. The planum on the left is assumed to have important speech-perception functions, and is generally larger than that on the right.

Planum parietale   Part of the cortex of the parietal lobe which surrounds the posterior end of the Sylvian fissure; the area in the right hemisphere is generally larger.

Polygyny   A mating system in which one male mates with several females.

Posterior   Referring to the back (e.g., of the brain).

Purdue Pegboard   A manual dexterity task requiring subjects to insert pegs in a row of holes—in some conditions, with the addition of small metal washers.

Pure tone threshold   The lowest sound level at which a single frequency can be heard. Usually, this is mapped for many separate frequencies.

Random sample   Subjects chosen from a population in a way that tries to avoid any bias in the selection.

Right-ear effect   The phenomenon in **dichotic listening** in which, when words are presented, those arriving at the right ear are reported more accurately than those arriving at the left ear, due to their favored access to the opposite left hemisphere.

Rod-and-Frame test   A rod must be placed into the vertical or horizontal position against a tilted background frame.

Rough-and-tumble play (play fighting)   The boisterous play of young males in which there is typically much body contact, but no harm is inflicted.

Scholastic Aptitude Tests (SAT)   A specific set of aptitude tests widely used for admission to colleges in the United States. The components include mathematics (SAT-M) and verbal (SAT-V) skills.

Self-selection   The idea that individuals may select certain activities or occupations because of their intrinsic abilities or interests. Contrasts with the idea that society determines the selection.

Sexually dimorphic nucleus of the preoptic area (SDN-POA)   This area of the hypothalamus is larger in male than in female rodents and has been shown to be influenced by early exposure to sex hormones.

Sex chromosomes   In humans, the 23rd pair of chromosomes; in females there are two Xs, and in males an X and a Y.

Sexual dimorphism   Originally used to describe the situation in which the sexes have different forms; now used more generally to describe any situation in which the sexes differ.

Sexual selection   The hypothesis that certain exaggerated characteristics in one sex (e.g., a rooster's comb) have been favored during evolution because the opposite sex found them attractive.

Spatial orientation   Refers to abilities that require corrections to be made for the orientation of an object in space, in order to solve a problem. For example, **mental rotation**.

Spatial visualization   Refers to abilities requiring some analysis of how an object has been manipulated (e.g., folded), in order to solve a problem. For example, the Paperfolding test.

Splenium   The most posterior part of the **corpus callosum**, the back section.

Standard deviation (SD)   The most commonly used measure of the variation of scores around the mean; the larger the SD, the greater the dispersal of scores from the mean.

Stereoscopic fusion   The combining of the two slightly different images that arrive at the two eyes, which creates the impression of depth; an important source of information about the distance of objects from us.

Symbol Digit test   See **Digit Symbol test**.

Tachistoscope   A device that can present a visual stimulus so briefly (lasting only fractions of a second), that the subject has no time to change direction of gaze. This allows presentation of a stimulus to only one visual field and therefore to one cerebral hemisphere.

Tamoxifen   A potential anti-estrogen that binds to intracellular estrogen receptors.

Targeting   Ability to throw a missile accurately at a specified target, as in dart throwing.

Testes   male **gonads**; in adults they are contained in the scrotum.

Testis-determining factor (TDF)   A factor assumed to be directed by the Y chromosome that determines that the bipotential gonad will become a **testis** instead of an **ovary**; the current candidate is the Sry gene.

Testosterone   The chief **androgen**, produced primarily by **testes**.

Transsexual An individual whose gender identity is not that of his or her chromosomal sex. Often such individuals are convinced for most of their lives that they are of the opposite sex, and using modern medical technology, may undergo a sex change even late in adulthood. This condition is not to be confused with homosexuality, which is a preference for a same-sex partner.

Turner's syndrome A genetic anomaly in which there is only one X on the 23rd chromosome set; the individual is **phenotypically** female, but usually sterile. Turner's syndrome individuals tend to have difficulty solving spatial and math problems.

Verbal fluency The ability to generate words quickly, with some constraint on the categories of words; most commonly it refers to the facility to generate words beginning with or containing a particular letter.

Water Level task The level of the water line must be drawn in a series of closed vessels tilted at various angles.

Wolffian ducts The embryonic ducts that have the potential to become the male internal reproductive system, forming the vas deferens and the seminal vesicles.

Author Index

Subject Index